A

Sports-

writer's

Life

Sports and American Culture Series
Bruce Clayton, Editor

A Sports-writer's Life

From the Desk of a
New York Times Reporter

Gerald Eskenazi

University of Missouri Press
Columbia and London

Copyright © 2003 by Gerald Eskenazi
University of Missouri Press, Columbia, Missouri 65201
Printed and bound in the United States of America
All rights reserved
5 4 3 2 1   07 06 05 04 03

Library of Congress Cataloging-in-Publication Data

Eskenazi, Gerald.
   A sportswriter's life : from the desk of a New York Times
reporter / Gerald Eskenazi.
         p. cm.   —   (Sports and American culture series)
      ISBN 0-8262-1510-6 (alk. paper)
   1. Eskenazi, Gerald. 2. Sportswriters—United States—
Biography. 3. Sports journalism—United States—
Authorship. I. Title. II. Series.
GV742.42.E75A3 2003
070.4'49796'092—dc22

                                        2003022016

∞ This paper meets the requirements of the
American National Standard for Permanence of Paper
for Printed Library Materials, Z39.48, 1984.

Designer: Kristie Lee
Typesetter: Crane Composition, Inc.
Printer and binder: Thomson-Shore, Inc.
Typefaces: Minion, Trixie

To the finest quartet ever conceived—

Corey Shuster, Alexa Eskenazi, Jordan Eskenazi and Jane Shuster.

Contents

Acknowledgments

To get to this point—the conceit of writing a memoir—I am indebted to someone who laughed at my stories of the day's, and night's, events, and seemed as excited as I was during the dips and twists of the writing business. That is my wife, Roz, of course, whose interest and enthusiasm made me believe that what I was doing actually was important.

I fed off her excitement for my assignments. If it mattered to her, I thought, then this must be big stuff. And she transmitted that same feeling—that their old man knew what he was doing and was somewhat of a big shot—to our three children: Ellen, Mark, and Mike. I think they all enjoyed this whole thing as much as I did.

One of them actually helped me assemble the following pages of this rollicking career. Mike Eskenazi seems to remember what I've done, where I've been, and what I've written a heck of a lot better than I do—and he wasn't even around for the first thirty-six years of my life.

As he helped me organize the years and the memories, I was struck by the impact they had on him—indeed, on all my children, and my wife, as well as on our friends. Or at least, enough of an impact so that Mike could recite back to me the bedtime war stories of my childhood and profession I used to tell him, Mark, and Ellen before tucking them in at night. These recollections made me realize even more how children hear everything we say.

I know of Mike's erudition, of course, and his sensibility. What I found indispensable in doing this book was his ability to cut through the words and pages and years to help organize chapters and events into a more cogent telling. He also pointed out to me where I could be more charitable in describing people, yet patted me on the back when there was a passage he particularly enjoyed.

Of course, any errors in memory or fact are mine since this is my take on a journalistic life and the profession I chose.

A book cannot be published without an editor who believes it is worthwhile and encourages the writer. Beverly Jarrett's immediate kind words and enthusiasm for what I have to say began this whole process, and John Brenner helped, quite expertly, to finish the job.

The larger "process," though, began back in Brooklyn, New York, where my mother understood a turn of phrase, and irony. At City College of New York, Professor Irving Rosenthal—who seems to have taught half the newspaper reporters in the city—imparted a respect for newspapers and a love for the well-written story. He never gave me a "10," but I don't believe anyone else ever got one, either.

Then I was fortunate to work for a succession of truly good and gifted people at the *New York Times,* starting with James Roach and then my "rabbi," James Tuite; and followed orders along the way from Sandy Padwe and Terry Taylor and Sandy Bailey and Joe Vecchione and Neil Amdur.

A Sports-writer's Life

1

The Written Word

Sometime back in the 1950s—probably in my second year at City College of New York, the school we proud poor kids thought of as the Harvard of the Proletariat—journalism turned into something beautiful to me.

Perhaps it was seeing my name in the school paper; perhaps it was learning about the exquisite torture of fitting a headline into its assigned space, or about the symmetry of layout. Somehow, despite our studies, despite the hours spent traveling to Brooklyn to a printer in Williamsburg under the rattling elevated train, the paper always came out twice a week, and it came out loud.

My romance with writing for newspapers began in the sixth grade, when I saw my name over a story in the class newsletter. That first byline leaped from the page, for it proclaimed that what followed below was official. I was an avid newspaper reader by then, and with this byline I had joined a fraternity of truth-tellers. People would read me to understand something. It was a wonderful responsibility.

By the time I got to college, I had accumulated a few journalistic notches, albeit on the high school paper with its twice-a-month feverish activity. But in college I suddenly joined a newspaper that was an endeavor, a shared, unpredictable, bumpy ride. Journalism consumed me.

Every day on the A train that took me from the streets of East New York, Brooklyn, all the way up to school in Harlem, forty-eight minutes that gave me a chance to read the *Daily News* and the *New York Times,* I searched these papers for their "look." I was enchanted by the bylines in the *Times*—Orville Prescott, Bosley Crowther, Brooks Atkinson, Drew Middleton, Arthur Krock, Harrison Salisbury. The names had a majesty, of course a WASP-ness, a rock-solid grounding in all that was right with the world.

And the *News*—my other world, the world of the back-page "Brooks," and Jackie, the Bronx Bombers, the Jints, of Dick Young, and Ed Sullivan, Danton Walker. A letters to the editor section called "The Voice of the People." A centerfold of stark photographs. The paper also looked good. It was a clean tabloid—column rules neatly around the photos, black headlines with lots of white space between them.

And then, one day after dropping out of City College for the third or fourth time, thanks to my penchant for eschewing homework in favor of the school paper—there would be more departures, to be sure, before I got my degree—I made my way up to the *New York Times.*

Why not? I had nothing else to do. I wasn't sure how far I ever would get in college. On that day in May 1959, for some reason, the paper actually had two openings for copy boys—one in news, one in sports. The man behind the desk doing the hiring asked me only one pertinent question: was I the editor-in-chief of the CCNY newspaper? I could answer yes, and I was offered the job.

But which one, for thirty-eight dollars a week?

I had a somewhat daunting image of the newsroom as the world's biggest editorial monster, where one could get lost. Sports, I thought, was a cozier location, where I might more readily show my stuff, my view of the way I thought journalism was headed. I chose sports.

Mostly, it was great fun, from May 26, 1959, until the day I retired, January 31, 2000. Along the way, I wrote more than eight thousand stories for the *Times,* many beyond the sports pages, in the book review, magazine, travel, and living sections. I continued doing pieces for the paper even after officially leaving—at retirement, I became a contract writer. Each of us was comfortable being around the other. It was not college, though, although it was at times what they told you journalism should be—a search for the story, and then writing it in a grand way so that you were happy and the reader was informed.

Toward the end of my stint, as the world (sports and the rest of it) moved at light-speed, as yesterday's possibilities became today's verities and yesterday's verities quickly became yesterday's news, I increasingly asked myself, what can we all learn from this spectacular journey?

There are signposts here: how journalism creeps into consciousness early, how the business evolves, how to get a story, what happened behind the words, "war" stories from the field, how a writer changes as society moves forward (or, in some cases, backward).

For me the *Times* has always had a majestic quality, even after I joined it and should have lost my awe. But there I was, a copy boy, just a few weeks into the job, when around midnight a professorial-looking fellow I instantly recognized from his thumbnail picture over his column in the *New York Post*—Murray Kempton—walked in. He seemed to belong at the *Times* more than he did at the *Post,* and he acted as if he knew everyone at the paper where I worked, and as if it should be the most natural thing in the world for him to show up there.

Kempton was one of the icons I grew up with when the *Post* was the paper my mother brought home from work every day—the passionately liberal paper of Max Lerner and Jimmy Cannon and Milton Gross and the political cartoonist Herblock. Kempton was a baseball Giants' fan, and the bastards had moved to California the year before. So for whatever reason—maybe he lived around Times Square—he would wander in late at night, walk over to the rear of the newsroom to the sports department facing 43rd Street, open the bell jar where the Western Union ticker was housed, and unravel the strand of paper, looking for the inning-by-inning account of his beloved Giants' game that day.

It is a memory I still cherish, along with the look and feel and smell of the place. As a copy boy I often had to bring messages to other departments, or move copy to the composing room, where the pages were put together. I explored other areas of the old building as well: old storerooms with the musty smell of yellowing newspapers; the crisp neatness of the Sunday offices all the way up on the eighth floor; the red-carpeted entrance to the publisher's office on the fourteenth, as high as you got at the *New York Times.*

Ah, the smell. The printing presses were in the sub-basement, in New York City bedrock so that the vibrations wouldn't make the building shudder. Sometimes after nine o'clock at night I would walk down a back stairwell to the press room from the third floor. I wanted to see and hear the presses. As I got closer to that sub-basement, the walls in the stairwell got blacker and the smell of ink was pervasive. Finally, when I got to the place where the printing presses were housed, the wall was inky. Touch the doorknob, and the ink came off. Then I'd walk back up, and the higher I got, the cleaner the air, and the walls and banister and stairs. By the time I got to the seventh or eighth floors, there was no ink at all on the walls.

But this was fantasy stuff for me. Over the years reality was what I lived with. While I believe I avoided the cynicism of many of my colleagues—and certainly of a growing number of fans, whose heroes' feet of clay have long ago crumbled—I discovered the sports world was nothing like the real world. In fact, the news department at the *Times* liked to derisively call us "the toy department." And yet all of us in the sportswriting business somehow conspired to make it something more— as if sports was a metaphor for life, when it really was a pale imitation.

Few of us today actually write stories from inside a newspaper office. And that, I believe, makes for a disconnect. Imagine what newspaper life was like when you were among others in the paper's environment:

You made a left out of the *New York Times*, walked diagonally across 43rd Street, and entered Gough's, the newspaperman's bar. Cigarette smoke smacked your nostrils when you first opened the door. Then the noise. A few feet inside was the bar, where men with printer's hats (formed out of the newspaper) sat alongside reporters. Money was on the bar, the change the bartender laid down after you paid for a drink. You never picked up that change until you were ready to leave. You were among honorable men. The bartender also cashed paychecks, and so every Wednesday at seven o'clock the pressmen and the writers and the printers brought in their yellow checks to be cashed, always leaving something for the bartender. In the back there was a restaurant—pork chops, scrambled eggs, macaroni and cheese—presided over by John the Waiter, a horse player.

Did Gough's make you a better writer, or pressman? Did the smoke, the booze, the guffaws, the stories, help you in the business? Well, of course they did. Just in the way barracks humor made you a better soldier, or fraternity hi-jinks made you a better collegian.

A lot of it was stupid and coarse. But you also became part of what had come before. I may have been a copy boy, but I was sitting next to and exchanging stories with Pulitzer Prize winners, or gray-haired, red-nosed printers who had been there since H. L. Mencken's heyday in the 1920s. I was in that stream that started when, of course, things were so much more fun. At least, that was what they told me.

In 1959 there still were three tabloids in the city, still the afternoon papers, still the Trib and the *Times*. Many of these fellows had been doing this since the twenties—the height of the tabloid wars, when head-busters from Moe Annenberg's Hearst newspapers went out in trucks, when fallen women with cigarettes dangling from their lips made Page One, when there were sob sisters and leg men and calls of "Get me rewrite!" Or so they liked to say. Still, when I began there were seven newspapers for seven constituencies, reporters wearing snap-brim fedoras. Buccaneers with typewriters, for the most part.

I already had tasted the newspaper business by the time I started working as a copy boy for that thirty-eight dollars a week. This was what they paid you for a Group 1 job at the *Times*—the same as messengers and elevator operators, which indicated the prestige I held. Reporters were Group 10. Two years earlier, back in 1957, I had a summer job at the *New York Mirror*—the home of Walter Winchell, Dear Abby, and a funny sports columnist named Dan Parker. I was Brooklyn-savvy and knew a trick or two—when I brought coffee to the reporters at the *Mirror*, I always made sure there were napkins and a stirrer and a few sugars in the bag as well.

"You'll go far," the city editor, a baldish guy with green eyeshades named Ed Markel, told me. "Smart guy," he added.

Success with the coffee run—as we called it—led to me being the *Mirror*'s Page One copy boy. I sat next to Markel as edition time got closer. They ran me off on little errands—picking up Winchell's copy, bringing "cuts," or photos, to the composing room. Then one day in July, we had a big breaking story. No, not the start of the landmark federal trial on integration in the South. The one about the actress Maureen O'Hara suing *Confidential* magazine, which had claimed she was necking in the balcony of Grauman's Chinese Theater with her "Latin Lover."

I went to the Page One conference.

"Which is it—Maureen or integration on Page One?" growled Bobby Hertzberg, the makeup editor. Markel thought for a bit.

"Integration," he said finally. "All caps. But put Maureen under it, upper- and lower-case, with a picture."

And this is how I came to cost the *Mirror* a fortune in circulation. I went to the composing room with Hertzberg, a red-haired, wisecracking newspaperman who must have seen too many movies about smart-ass newspapermen. The fellow making up Page One—known as a "printer"—took the "cut," the head shot of Maureen O'Hara, and tried to fit it into the hole designed for it. It was about an eighth of an inch too long.

"Take this cut to the photoengravers," Hertzberg told me, "and have 'em slice this much off it. But make sure you do it off the top of her head—don't cut the bosom."

Well, of course the guy I took the picture to put it in the wrong way. He sliced the boobs, not the hair. When I brought it to Hertzberg, he contemplated the shorter bust of Maureen, turned the cut over in his fingers and growled, "Kid, you just cost us a hundred thousand readers."

So that was part of my journalism history when I finally settled in at the *Times* a few years later.

The place was more placid than the *Mirror,* had more of a sense that what was happening today would, to some degree, still be happening tomorrow. At the tabloid *Mirror* you were engulfed in the moment—that day's rape, or liquor-store robbery, or bookie bust, was the most important thing in your world. Part of that immediacy, I'm sure, came because of proximity—everyone in the cramped newsroom at the *Mirror* was touching. The *Times,* on the other hand, was spread out—and some of the departments weren't even on the same floor. The Sunday section virtually had the eighth floor to itself. In fact, the editor of the entire Sunday operation was an ancient ruler named Lester Markel, and the eighth floor was his fiefdom. The third-floor newsroom sprawled from 43rd to 44th Streets, taking up almost all of the block between Broadway and Eighth Avenue.

So this was my new world.

It was a world that was still decades away from computers, but not talk of "automation," a dreaded electronic breakthrough that was to move the newspaper's hardware—the presses and linotypes—out of the

1890s and eventually into oblivion. It would result in a new way of look-ing at paper, or the lack of it, at typing (words appear on a screen, not in black on white paper). It was to create a new sort of newspaperman, who increasingly was a newspaperwoman.

But there was something so cozy about the old ways. You didn't have to think too much about morality, especially in sportswriting. You didn't have to worry about responsibility, so go ahead and throw back that drink at six, while your copy waited until seven.

At least, this is what I saw. I went to bars, but I was not a drinker. Just as, say, I went to the indoor polo matches at the Sixty-ninth Regiment Armory but was not a polo player. I learned quickly that when you're a sportswriter, you're an observer. And there should be the foul line, or the baseline, or the sideline between you and the athlete or the coach.

The newspapermen of my early days loved to talk about their mo-ments with athletes. These dialogues took place after hours, in bars, hotel lobbies, restaurants, the track. Never at the theater. One man from this genre, Jerry Mitchell of the *New York Post,* was a perpetually rum-pled, sweating, overweight clever guy with a fine sense of humor, a good dinnertime companion. He also roomed on one train ride in spring training with the Indians' Satchel Paige, the larger-than-life forty-five-year-old rookie who had finally made it to the big leagues when a few other blacks charged into the suddenly opened door behind Jackie Robinson. Mitch told me of getting back to the train late one night at a whistle-stop somewhere in Arizona (the Indians used to barnstorm with the Giants in that state since most baseball teams did their training camps in Florida).

"I opened the door to the compartment—I had the lower berth—and Satch says to me, 'Hey, come back later, I got my wife in here with me.' That Paige, I found out later—he had a 'wife' in every town."

"Cronyism," the revered columnist Walter Lippmann said, "is the curse of the newspaperman." Well, then, a lot of newspapermen—espe-cially sportswriters—were cursed. But you knew that already. Imagine Tom Brokaw sharing a hotel room with a presidential adviser. OK, so Jerry Mitchell of the *New York Post* rooming with Satchel Paige isn't on the same cosmic level. But it was part of the us-we world that sports-writers inhabited.

Early in my stint at the *Times,* the fellow who had covered the Yankees since the 1920s, John Drebinger, retired. Drebbie was almost deaf. When he spoke on the telephone, he placed the earpiece on his chest—that's where his hearing-aid amplifier was. He spoke in guffaws, and loud, because he couldn't hear himself.

The story about his deafness was legendary: how at a cocktail party everyone was chowing down and talking and making noise, and he was in the midst of telling a story about some amorous adventure. Then, as sometimes happens, there was a lull and the room was fairly quiet. At that moment, Drebbie hit his listeners with the story's punchline, which, in his deafness, he shouted out: "In the confusion," he screamed, "I fucked the widow." And that is why, every once in a while in the *New York Times,* you will read a sentence by the blithe columnist, Dave Anderson, that begins, "In the confusion . . ."

Anyway, at Drebinger's retirement party, Ralph Houk, the Yankees' general manager, addressed the writers. "I wish you younger fellows could be more like Drebbie," suggested Houk. "After all, we're all in this together."

And so they were, at least in Houk's time. The newer writers were a new breed, labeled "Chipmunks" by the *Post's* Jimmy Cannon. I loved reading Cannon, especially one-liners he produced in a column he called "Nobody Asked Me, But . . ."One of his memorable sentences was this: "Nothing improves a starlet's diction like marrying money." Cannon also was on to something when he came up with the "Chipmunks" sobriquet. Yet Cannon was no Establishment-type. He didn't have knee-jerk reactions to the longings of athletes to get a fair shake, and he was no automatic friend of management. But he was older, and so one day, in a fit of his usually splenetic outpourings, he brought together all the younger writers under one banner.

It was at a baseball game at Yankee Stadium (and what more fitting place for the old verities). Phil Pepe of the *Telegram,* an outgoing guy who had two prominent front teeth, was there. That much we know. Over the years other writers have said they were there as well (and for all I know, could have been): Maury Allen, Stan Isaacs, Steve Jacobson, Leonard Shecter, Larry Merchant, George Vecsey. These men had replaced the beat writers who had been in their posts for fifteen or twenty or thirty years. Cannon by then—this was perhaps 1962—had moved to the *Journal-American*. He heard these new guys chattering among themselves, laughing when they should have been serious, and he said, "You guys . . . you guys," then glanced at Pepe and completed the sentence: "You're like a bunch of chipmunks."

That title was given even finer symbolism and significance following Game 7 of the 1962 World Series between the Yankees and San Francisco Giants. In the postgame frenzy of interviews, Ralph Terry, the Yankees' winning pitcher, was summoned to the telephone while talking to several reporters. When he returned, Isaacs asked who had called him.

"My wife, she called to congratulate me," said Terry.

"What was she doing?" asked Isaacs.

"Feeding the baby," said Terry.

"Breast, or bottle?" asked Isaacs.

That was the question that separated the old from the new journalists—not "What pitch did you throw him on 3-and-2?" The "why" and the "id" and the "ego" became a part of reporting. "Breast or bottle?" The old-timers were incredulous, even angry. The new breed was ecstatic. Finally, a question of importance at a World Series game. Until then, sportswriters rarely went to locker rooms to interview players after the game.

"Why should I?" asked an old-timer, Joe King of the *Telegram*. "None of those pricks can speak English anyway."

By the time I got to the press box, Cannon and Gross and even Winchell were on the way out, working for other papers, bemoaning the young jackals who were making fun of them. I had wanted to know these legendary writers, but the Chipmunks made you feel as if you were some sort of retro fool by actually chatting with Cannon. Not that Cannon was easy. Everything was about his comfort, and his plumbing.

Once, after a fight in Philadelphia between Joe Frazier and Oscar Bonavena (who was to be murdered in a Nevada brothel some years later), Dave Anderson was giving us a ride back to the city. It was a cold night, so Cannon asked me to sit in the back seat of the car.

"I've got to sit in the front near the heater," he explained. "My prostate needs the warmth." Eventually, he turned the heat off and I shivered in the back. It was getting too warm for him, he claimed. This from the man who used to go to Toots Shor's with DiMaggio and Hemingway.

Cannon wasn't the only icon who turned out to be a pain in person: one of the major columnists who bridged both that 1940s and 1960s world was Dick Young. But increasingly he was getting angry at these new long-haired writers, and especially their stand on Vietnam. Young was against unionism for players, he was for the sanctity of contracts (until he broke his own with the *News* to jump to the *Post*), he was for old-fashioned integrity and patriotism. At the Opening Ceremonies at the Olympics in Lake Placid, I heard a voice behind me shout, "Way to go, Jerry!" as he complimented me for singing along with the National Anthem. It was Young.

But that instant of approval failed to overshadow another moment involving Young. It was at the 1976 American League championship at Yankee Stadium. Chris Chambliss had just hit a home run against the Royals to propel the Yankees to the World Series. Fans stormed the field, creating exactly the havoc that Young, the conservative curmudgeon, had always railed against. Once he had moaned in print, "What are they doing to my America?" as the anti-Establishment types proliferated. Now I stood in a reporters' line in front of Young as we waited to enter the jubilant Yankee locker room. A worker from the stadium's caterer passed by with a cart filled with champagne. He was headed for the locker room and the usual victory dousing party. He stopped next to me. The media line was so thick he couldn't pass us. We could hear the fans still in the park shouting and blowing horns and police trying to stop them from tearing up the grass field while Chambliss had to be escorted through a vortex of back-slappers. It was the Armageddon Young had feared.

Young looked inside the box the waiter was carrying. Then he put his hand in and pulled out a bottle of champagne. He put it into his attaché case.

"What are you doing?" asked the workman.

"What the fuck's it to you?" retorted Young, the American.

That petty theft aside, Young to his credit had been one of the first sportswriters to leave the coziness of the press box after games and go to the locker room to actually talk to ballplayers about what they had done. Television eventually forced all the reporters down to the locker room. The readers at home already knew the score and the details and, with instant replay, even knew how and why. What they didn't know, however, were the players' feelings. Or whether their fathers ever played catch with them or whether their mothers breast- or bottle-fed them.

The Chipmunks were not going to be sharing any Pullmans with ballplayers. In fact, they'd be exposing what went on behind closed doors. They were abetted in this endeavor by ballplayers such as Jim Bouton, whose book *Ball Four* angered Mickey Mantle and Whitey Ford and Yogi Berra to such an extent that Bouton, a onetime twenty-game winner, wasn't invited to Yankee Old-Timers' games for more than thirty years, until the end of the 1990s.

There were many ways that, in Houk's naive but heartfelt words, "we were all in this together." In baseball, the official scorer was a beat writer who got paid for his scoring service by the local team. The harness-racing writers—and every paper had at least one as well as a handicapper (except for the *Times*)—wrote for the daily programs at Yonkers and Roosevelt raceways. The writers got paid by the tracks for these pieces.

One night in Montreal during a Stanley Cup hockey playoff series, I went out to dinner with my *Times* colleague, Bob Lipsyte, and Neil Offen of the *Post*. The check came and I suggested, of course, that we divide it three ways. "Don't be silly," said Offen. "I'll pick it up." When we protested, Offen explained, "The Rangers are paying for it."

And so they did. The New York Rangers had told the *Post* to send a reporter and they'd pay his airfare and hotel bill and pick up the food tab. It would be good for hockey, the Rangers explained. And anyway, the *Post*—socialist on the editorial page—was a notoriously cheapskate outfit with its own workers, especially when it came to hockey, the fourth sport in a four-sport town.

I may have been a young, barely visible reporter in the late 1960s, but of course I worked for the prestigious *Times*. So without even asking, I got free season's tickets for the Jets, the Knicks, and the Rangers. Just like that. I had a card that got me into general admission for Giants' football games for fifty cents. My baseball writers' card got me into the press box at Yankee Stadium or Shea Stadium whenever I wanted. Before long, I learned that if your second name was "New York Times" you were granted an immediate title—something like a prince of the realm. But every sportswriter in New York had cachet in certain quarters.

You could go to Leone's for lunch on Mondays with the hockey writers and spend five dollars in a specially set-up back room, where the maitre d' would ply you with gourmet breads and veal dishes and end with plates heavy with fruit and cheese, along with some wine. Or you could do the same at Leone's on Tuesdays with the track writers.

Baseball? Football? No problem. The teams served extensive pregame meals. The Giants were especially noted for their rice pudding. The Yankees had an old-fashioned bar equipped with bartender.

There was a copy editor at the paper who knew where every free or cheap meal was hidden, and he made them all. We called him Sir Lunch-a-Lot. If you wanted to eat out with your wife or friends on Friday or Saturday nights, simply call Roosevelt or Yonkers raceways and get a steak dinner—everything included—in the glass-enclosed dining rooms overlooking the tracks. For free. If you were working and couldn't avail yourself of the formal dining room, no problem. One area of the Roosevelt Raceway dining room was set aside for working reporters. It was called "Cohen's Corner," in honor of a *Post* reporter, Leonard Cohen.

The tracks also ran huge media-oriented dinners at Manhattan hotels and Long Island estates, in the middle of Gatsby country. Often, a B-list celebrity was on hand. That is how I came to interview Jayne Mansfield, who turned out to be smart and something more than a Marilyn Monroe knockoff. Ms. Mansfield was paraded around a harness-racing dinner as if she were a prize mare. So in the spirit of the evening, and knowing she had absolutely no knowledge of the sport, I asked her if she knew the difference between a trotter and a pacer.

"No," she replied in her starlet's breathy voice. "But as long as the horses do, isn't that what's important?" How could I argue with that?

When there was a newspaper strike in 1962, Yonkers Raceway hired me and a bunch of other writers who had done stories on harness racing. Our assignment? Stuff photos of Adios, the great standardbred sire, into envelopes to send to fans enamored of the stud. Our salary was fifty-five dollars a week, which was, I think, as much as the paper had been paying me.

None of us thought this was unusual—indeed, many of my older colleagues believed they had it coming since they had been so nice to the track in so many ways. I say this not to point fingers or, from the altitude of time, to look down at the way things were in my business. These were facts, part of a culture that learned in a tribal way—stories handed down, old telling the young. The older guys who had shown me the ropes—well, maybe they were from the Depression generation, maybe they had a sense of entitlement as newspapermen, maybe they earned so little that a steak dinner made them affluent for the night. I don't think you found many college degrees among the rank-and-file reporters when I broke in.

The freebie world of the newspaperman—and thus, the camaraderie between the reporter and the people and teams he wrote about—changed forever in the 1970s with two unrelated events: Watergate, and a story in *New York Magazine.*

Watergate, and the subsequent book and film, *All the President's Men,* helped make journalism an honored profession again. Suddenly, bright high school seniors wanted to become communications majors (a mistake, I always lecture them; make communications a minor part of your college courses). Still, newspapers were seen as the truth-makers. Why, they could bring down a prevaricating president. When in history had a president responded to a question by claiming, "I am not a crook"? This is what journalists could do.

Meanwhile, *New York Magazine,* a smart, media-oriented weekly that had boasted at one time writers such as Jimmy Breslin, Dick Schaap, Judith Crist, and John Simon, ran a huge piece that had been promoted by a self-serving Madison Square Garden. It detailed all the free tickets everyone in the news media—mostly sportswriters—received to the Knicks and Rangers games. It even included a seating chart. The Garden had wanted to get rid of all these hangers-on and figured, rightly, that an exposé would get the public and the newspapers to do something about it. Never mind that the Garden had willingly proffered the tickets in the first place. The Knicks and Rangers were becoming hot-ticket items, and there was no easy way to say to a reporter, "Give us back your seats."

It is fair to say that when the *Times* saw the list of reporters who had all these free seats it was "shocked, shocked," in the words of the cynical police inspector in *Casablanca* when he hears of corruption. Several New York City tabloids, I suspect, were less shocked. But the *Times* and most of the other major papers across the United States did something about it immediately. I know that my paper looked into all the various ways reporters may be influenced by sources or organizations they write about—from free tickets, to Christmas gifts, to plane travel, to the use of cars.

First, memos sprouted from various editors' offices about not taking tickets. Then, lengthier looks at the whole practice of newspaper entitlement produced longer statements on ethics and about keeping arm's-length distances from those we write about. The *Times* even generated a letter to be sent out at Christmastime to all the advertisers we did business with, as well as teams and Broadway producers: thanks, but we don't accept gifts. And if you were the recipient of a gift, sent inadvertently, of course, why, the *Times* invited its reporters to bring it in, and the paper's mail room would ship it back with a lovely thanks-but-no-thanks note attached.

This new morality had a tremendous, positive effect on the business. Most important, it forced many reporters, especially sportswriters, to think of themselves as professionals and not free-loaders. This, in turn, forced organizations and teams to look at reporters in a different way as well. Thus, the Yankees and the Mets no longer dole out free pregame meals. You pay seven dollars or so. But we have our integrity as a result. Of course, this also had some unintended consequences: George Steinbrenner invited the *Times*'s executive editor, A. M. Rosenthal, and his top deputy to a Yankees' game and naturally to sit in the owner's private box behind home plate. Rosenthal insisted on paying for a seat—even though there were no seats for sale in the suite. And some newspapers, such as the *Washington Post,* simply stopped the practice of traveling with teams because the clubs would not charge the reporters for the airfare. The clubs explained that if they did, that would create a whole set of problems with federal rules regarding charters. However, this narrowed the access reporters had to players. There's nothing like the relaxed time on an airplane flight to have a heart-to-heart talk with a coach, an owner, or a player.

Eventually, every major organization in America became aware of what reporters could and could not take—no tickets for Disney World; no free hotels or airline seats; no Broadway shows. Indeed, the *Times* even stopped its reporters from buying desirable "house seats" at the theater, on the presumption that this was a favor Broadway was doing for the newspaper.

Then the paper prohibited reporters collaborating on books with people they might write about. This, too, was a perfectly valid request, long overdue. How could you be sharing a book advance with a pitcher, or an actress, and then write about them objectively in a newspaper? This soon extended to the time-honored system of newspaper people voting for awards. The paper forbade any of its columnists from voting for various theatrical or film honors on the theory it could be a conflict of interest—or at least, could impact our ability to get objective stories. If you did not vote for one actor, say, he might not grant you an interview.

Then one day one of the deputy managing editors met with some of us in sports to tell us we no longer could vote for the Baseball Hall of Fame. The reasoning was the same. We didn't want to get, say, Yogi Berra teed off with us because we didn't vote for one of his buddies. And anyway, the paper reasoned, it's not a newspaper reporter's job to vote for anything. It's his or her job to tell a story, well and honestly. Thus, the paper soon respectfully requested that we also not attend political rallies as advocates if we write about politics, or wear buttons proclaiming our favorite politicians.

To the degree that I had been one of the recipients of free tickets, I had a role in this new morality. I hope a lot of reporters thank me for inadvertently raising the integrity bar. I suspect some would not.

My generation not only bridged a transition of the craft of sportswriting but also asked a deeper set of questions. And yet, we were still sharing with the old-timers the same athletes. Consider the stars of their time when I broke in: baseball's Ted Williams, Mickey Mantle, Willie Mays; basketball's Wilt Chamberlain, Bob Cousy; football's Jim Brown, Frank Gifford; boxing's Floyd Patterson; hockey's Jean Beliveau, Gordie Howe; tennis's Ken Rosewall, Billie Jean King; horse racing's

Eddie Arcaro, Ted Atkinson. Pantheon names—yet some newer types were coming along, sporting long hair, some even making fun of their older managers or coaches. In fact, whole teams like this were on the horizon: the Mets, the Jets. The Yankee Clipper did not understand what Simon and Garfunkel meant when they sang, "Where have you gone, Joe DiMaggio?"

"I haven't gone anywhere," he told friends. "I've been here all the time."

But the new writers and the new athletes got it. It didn't come easily, either to the old or the new. If there was one person of the sixties who catalyzed the final break with the past in sportswriting, who coalesced the new against the old, it was Muhammad Ali. He created a rift not only in sportswriting but in America as well.

2

The End of Reporting as We Know It

Until Ali, we journalists rarely applied layers of observation to our athletes: the people we wrote about were either good or bad, a thug or a prince, a lady or . . . well, we didn't really write about the other kind in sports. Dempsey either was a punk or a hail-fellow-well-met. Ted Williams (my idol, by the way) was either The Kid or a surly rascal who refused to tip his cap to fans and who once spit toward the press box. Joe Louis, of course, always was Mr. Nice Guy. DiMaggio? As *Life* once noted in a simpler era, he was an Italian who took care to smell nice, using scented hair cream. The dour Sonny Liston was a thug; the shy Floyd Patterson was the good guy.

On the one hand we have the political considerations that inform sportswriting these days. You virtually cannot ignore political correctness; you create a sociological issue that this is the *first*—woman, black, Hispanic, over-fifty-year-old—to accomplish a certain feat. Witness the insistence of the mainstream press to make something unusual about Tiger Woods's success because he has a black father. Or of the *New York Times* asking Woods in an editorial to lead the battle to bring women members into the Augusta National Golf Club. I'm writing this at a moment in time when we scorecard race in America to see how good we are: it is a sort of litmus test for society. But the Stanford-educated Woods refuses to allow himself to be typecast (he points out his mother is a Thai) and he does not refer to himself as a black. Yet almost every

17

time he wins an event, we in the media still put a racial spin on it. It is almost as if this is something of a victory for . . . what? Inclusion? The American Dream? The ghetto kid? None of this has anything to do with Tiger Woods, of course.

We excuse the inexcusable—the Yankees' Roger Clemens throws a spearlike shard of a broken bat at Mike Piazza of the Mets in a World Series game? So what? Clemens was in a "zone." Patrick Ewing, a married man with three children hauling down a few million a year, is the beneficiary of oral sex in an Atlanta nightclub owned by a mob-connected figure? No big deal. So did Dennis Rodman and others. Almost 20 percent of the players in the NFL draft have their names on police blotters? The gag in Boulder, Colorado, was that the police drove around with a team picture of the University of Colorado football squad because of the repeated incidents of rape, burglary, and general nastiness. They all were big stories, for a while. Then silence. Isn't there something more we should know? Isn't there some basic problem here? Why did this become merely a one-day story?

This is an odd dichotomy. For in the writing business these days, we have been reduced to an Oprah Winfrey–Jerry Springer–Phil Donahue–Ricki Lake mode of reporting: instant noise, with no resolution. We are whetting the appetite of an audience grown caffeinated with the likes of the magazine-style TV shows. Causes get taken up, some poor soul, or evil-doer, becomes infamous, and then fades away. Thus, the story that affected, oh, maybe seven people became front-page news when the hide-bound Augusta National Golf Club stiffened its stance on not having women members. Golf is national news two or three times a year, during the Masters or United States Open (and increasingly when Tiger Woods does something no golfer had ever accomplished before). And that's it, until Martha Burk, a feminist activist with an eclectic assortment of constituents (her National Council of Women's Organizations included both NOW and a group trying to get better wages for housemaids), wrote a letter in the summer of 2002 to the head of Augusta, a fellow named William W. Johnson, nicknamed "Hootie." The letter seemed to Johnson a form of extortion—admit women, or else—and he went public with the letter. Until then, who among us had even known Burk's group had been lobbying to have a woman enter the club?

Over the next six months, the *New York Times* wrote thirty-seven sto-ries—an average of more than one a week—about the issue. The *Washington Post* added thirty-two of its own. It became, however, the *Times*'s story, a crusade unprecedented in the sports section and that at times seemed to rival the zeal with which the news side of the paper went after the Watergate scandals thirty years earlier. The *Times* even asked Tiger Woods in an editorial to use his considerable influence to force the issue at the club. He demurred.

It is an interesting issue—perhaps on a theoretical level. It makes for good journalism discussion. But it also is typical of what happens in so much sportswriting today. A broader social implication is attached to a story that no one is talking about, and suddenly everyone is talking about the issue, forgetting that for the most part they don't even care about the event. The *Times* grabbed this story as its own and led the re-porting of it, giving it an importance that transcended the real interest of the pages' readers. Of course, I understand that a newspaper does not necessarily have a pure obligation to give the people what they want—there is some obligation to address important issues, and the truth as it perceives it, even if readers aren't clamoring for it.

I wondered what the National Council of Women's Organizations would have thought about other issues of equal access—for example, letting me in the locker room (at women's sporting events). After all, women reporters routinely entered the men's lair.

Yes, there are big stories out there. But increasingly, issues arise out of small events—often because unsophisticated news people are latching onto them and think they have something big.

Does anyone ever wonder why a Las Vegas oddsmaker named Jimmy "The Greek" Snyder should have been a nationwide cause célèbre be-cause of his anthropological take on the black athlete? What was Jimmy the Greek, whose regular gig was on CBS giving odds on football games, doing explaining history? The answer surprises some people.

It was Super Bowl week, and the Redskins were led by the first black quarterback to get to the big game. A Washington, D.C., television an-nouncer—who happened to be black—was out in the field asking celeb-rities about the significance of the game. So where does this television newshound go for interviews?—to a cozy place, indoors. To Duke Zei-bert's restaurant, a hangout for politicians and newspapermen—Harry

Truman and J. Edgar Hoover had been regulars. And who does the reporter spot? Jimmy the Greek, who had downed a few drinks, having dinner. Jimmy the Greek? Why would anyone care what he had to say on race—and why would you even ask him?

But because the Greek was in the vicinity of a camera and microphone, he was asked about the black athlete. The Greek's reply: "The black is a better athlete because he was bred to be that way." He also spoke about slave owners favoring men and women with big thighs, which led the *Times*'s George Vecsey to describe this as the "Jimmy the Greek School of Genetics." Of course, the Greek was dismissed from his two-hundred-thousand-dollars-a-year CBS job, which freed him to pursue his other interest in bloodlines—habituating racetracks.

It is unfathomable that a peripheral member of show business (or the media, or whatever category Jimmy fit into) was asked his take on race in America, and then that his explication was given such exposure—supposedly indicating how the rest of us Americans viewed blacks. Serious pundits commented on this as proof of lingering racism in America. But that is the easy way taken by so many on television. It's as if merely being in the public eye gives you a greater insight into serious issues, so you get on the tube.

This "gotcha" mentality bit the hapless Los Angeles Dodgers' general manager, Al Campanis. Campanis was asked by Ted Koppel on *Nightline* about the dearth of black managers in baseball in a program celebrating the fortieth anniversary of Jackie Robinson's major-league debut. Who better than Campanis, a former teammate of Robinson's when they were minor leaguers?

Here is what virtually no one knew: Campanis had been one of the sport's leaders back in the segregated 1940s in befriending black ballplayers and then eventually hiring many of them to play for the Dodgers. Indeed, he was almost a heroic figure of that period. But he was hardly a sociologist, nor did he hold a master's in syntax or locution, although he had attended New York University. He also did not know his physiology. So he said something about black ballplayers "lacking the necessities" to manage. What did he mean? Did he mean the experience? Did he mean the smarts? He compounded his muddled statement by talking about blacks not being good swimmers because of a buoyancy factor. Koppel gave Campanis several chances to reevaluate his statements. But

Campanis, who was well-known to reporters for getting snagged on the barbs of language, merely entangled himself further. He resigned a few days later.

I believe that sportswriting has fallen prey to this easy way out. We have finally turned into the embodiment of what Walter Lippmann, who had a knack for saying these things, once decried—that reporters write about the wart on the face of society. Thus, the score of a game these days invariably takes second fiddle to some bizarre aspect of the game, or some undercurrent of the story. Fact-checking, getting comments that matter, interviewing techniques—often these are subverted to the demands of the moment.

Here is the advice I was given when I went out to do my first baseball story: get the score in the first paragraph.

Imagine—and I am using the *Times* as a paradigm, perhaps unfairly—that in the body of every baseball story we wrote back in the fifties and sixties we even had to mention the name of the team's manager and what league the team was in. But what this gave the reader, and the writer, was a sense of weight, that this story had some official standing in the world of the printed word. Now, of course, everyone knows the score because of television, and everyone knows what odd aspect of the game has been detailed, replayed numerous times. This is not necessarily bad, but it has sidetracked the aim of the newspaper story. Editors are reluctant to go with a straightforward account, especially if it minimizes something that has been shown repeatedly on television. It is almost as if we, the writers, now must expand upon what the television news shows say about the events we are covering. Television drives the newspaper report.

In the midst of all this television-newspaper turmoil, along came Ali. He was the first athlete I had ever been around who seemed to revel in his celebrity status. He'd say something clever, then he'd peer over to see what you were writing. He enjoyed sparring with the gray-haired and baldish among my colleagues—with the irreverent, America-for-Americans Dick Young of the *Daily News,* with Cannon, with all the writers and columnists of any stripe. But he seemed especially to talk the most to those he perceived as doubting him, both as a fighter and as a political animal.

I thought he was a womanizing bigot.

Me and Muhammad Ali, at a news interview in 1966.

Yet because so many sportswriters—no, make that journalists over-all—were caught up in the turgid drama surrounding Vietnam, which coincided with much of the Civil Rights movement, he became the symbol of the right-thinking young man who finally, publicly, said what so many of us thought, "I ain't got no quarrel with them Vietcong." True enough. Add to the mix the fact that he was a black man, and that this country was really only months removed from Jim Crow laws, and it is easy to see how and why he became a sympathetic figure. So we in the business glossed over his cruelty to Joe Frazier, whom he called an

"Uncle Tom" and a "gorilla" because Frazier was an uncomplicated, non-political guy from Philadelphia who had no axe to grind. Or we quickly forgot after Ali taunted and wrecked Floyd Patterson in the ring, "Like a little boy tearing the wings off a butterfly, piecemeal," in the words of my colleague Bob Lipsyte. With each whomp, the taller, heavier Ali shouted at Patterson, "What's my name?" because Patterson had refused to call him "Ali" instead of "Clay."

The final guilt-ridden paroxysm of the media regarding Ali came that moment in Atlanta, when the Olympic lights shone on him and he lifted the Olympic torch to light the flame for the Games.

While I have—still—mixed emotions about Ali, I must admit that I wrote several stories that may have been helpful to him in rehabilitating his image. For I was a young—OK, altruistic, too—reporter when he was barred from fighting in New York State. That was the most important athletic commission in the country, if not the world, and it had barred him because he was a convicted felon—he had refused to take the step forward to be inducted into the army.

But here's what I uncovered: that while the State Athletic Commission had kicked out Ali as champion, it had recognized and allowed to continue to fight a convicted rapist, a fellow who served time for manslaughter, and a host of others who, really, were simply the kinds of guys who always made their living in the prize ring. When my story came out that the state had adopted this double standard, Ali soon was reinstated. Because of this early prejudice against him, because Ali's anti-war stance had resonated so deeply among the younger reporters (the older ones, including our own Arthur Daley, refused to call him "Ali" until he was almost an icon), he got a free pass as the years went on.

He would play the race card in Zaire against the plodding George Foreman, aligning himself with Africans as if they could relate to him, and he was able to get away with anti-white slurs against some of his opponents, while his pals in the so-called Black Muslim movement made money off him. He gave away about a third to his church. (His manager was Elijah Muhammad's son. A federal law, in effect because Joe Louis had lost so much money to his handlers, decreed fighters don't have to give more than a third of their earnings to their managers.)

But another anti-societal fighter did not have to loudly proclaim his devotion to Islam to enjoy the backing of many leaders. When Mike

Tyson was let out of prison for his rape conviction, he was thrown a party in Harlem at Sylvia's, the noted soul-food eatery.

This was the scene: a block party, with Tyson being honored by Uptown notables such as Basil Paterson, former Manhattan borough president; former Mayor David Dinkins; and the publisher of the *Amsterdam News*. The proceedings unfolded under the menacing glare of the Fruit of Islam, the bodyguards, many of whom learned their security skills in prison.

There was no dithering by Paterson or the others; they simply honored Tyson. When I asked Paterson why, I was told he was a "role model." Also, Paterson told me, "He served his time." Wasn't there someone there to say, "Wait a minute. This is obscene"? Shouldn't my great newspaper have been taken aback by the scene? Instead, I was one of two *Times* reporters sent to do the story, which came out vanilla and with no irony.

Of course, this was fairly late in the game, in the 1990s. The breakthroughs in reporting on Ali and race had come more than thirty years before, especially by Lipsyte. To an uncomfortable editor, Lipsyte wrote pieces detailing Ali's conversion to Islam (announced the day after he won the world championship from the brute Liston), and Lipsyte insisted on calling him "Ali." Other writers, such as Young, would begin their questions to him with, "Cassius . . ."

Ali confused us all, especially me. He could be charming, playful, as when he spoke of the need to economically empower black America.

"Look at the Jews in Miami Beach," he said to me in his dressing room before a fight. "They were barred from Miami Beach, so what did they do? They bought the place."

True enough, I thought. But Ali wondered whether he had gone over an imaginary line.

"You're not Jewish, are you?" he asked me. When I told him, yes, his delightful reply was, "Oops." I told him I wasn't offended, but he seemed embarrassed that he had indeed caused offense. Then he went out and picked apart another fighter.

Ali alternated between being engaging and sneering, and that confused many of us who wrote about him. How to depict him? What was

An interview with Joe Louis, 1970.

his true center? Was he the exuberant young man who one day decided to drive us all by bus up to the Catskills to shill for a fight he was going to be broadcasting? This was in 1965, he was the champ, and he was recuperating from a hernia operation, which kept him sidelined. Two leading contenders, Floyd Patterson and George Chuvalo, were going to meet in an elimination bout to face him. We were all headed for Chuvalo's training camp.

About forty of us boarded the media bus from Midtown, along with the driver. It was a red-and-white bus, with "World's Champ" lettered on the side. As soon as we got out of New York City and onto the New York State Thruway, Ali ("Cassius" still to most of the people on the bus) took over. He drove uneventfully for ninety minutes. And then, suddenly, with a jerk, we were all at a list as the bus nearly tumbled over. The road had narrowed and Ali had driven us into a ditch. The bus was tilted so far to the right that we couldn't get out the door. So someone opened an emergency exit on the left side and we all trudged out into the snow. We walked the half mile to the hotel.

Ali was contrite—a little boy caught being naughty. Still, he defended his driving. He claimed he drove the bus all the time. I asked him whether he had a license to drive a bus, and he said no. I asked him whether or not he even had a license, and he told me, "It was suspended. Too many points."

Anyway, we all got our stories written. The bus had been righted and brought back to the hotel. Ali didn't drive this time. But when we got to Manhattan, Ali suddenly got up and told the driver he wanted to get behind the wheel. Then he drove the bus through Harlem. He came up to a bus stop, where people saw this red-and-white bus slowly pull alongside. Then Ali opened the door and said to the waiting people, "Who's the greatest?" They were too stunned to realize what was happening. He drove along some more, then spotted a teenager walking down 125th Street. Ali stopped the bus again. He opened the door. The youngster looked at Ali as if in a dream, and said, "The Champ!"

Ali symbolized the dilemma of the newspaper business for me. I was repelled, yet attracted. I laughed loudly, then reluctantly, at his antics. I felt empathy for his struggle, anger at his cronies.

All the while, I was, I see now, struggling with my past as well, for I had grown up at a time when I knew no one who was black, except a woman who occasionally cleaned our house. "The girl," as my grandmother called her, was a cheerful woman probably in her forties whose name was Mary. My grandmother, as I'm sure white women everywhere in the neighborhood did, made sure to put the liquor and silverware in hard-to-find places when the cleaning girl came.

I'm not sure my grandmother singled out blacks for this odious behavior. The Irish, the Italians, the Poles would have come under the same scrutiny. Since everyone on my block, and everyone across the street, was Jewish—in fact for blocks around it was a Jewish world, with an Italian family scattered here and there—I had virtually no contact with a black person as a peer until high school.

Yet—there were stories to be written once I became a reporter. Objective stories, but obviously from my viewing point. In the newspaper business we talk about objectivity. That's simply a theory. Truthfully, every story—a burning building, a soccer game, the secretary of state's news conference—is written from a perspective. How could it not be? Once a story is filtered through Reporter A, it will come out different from the one that was seen by Reporter B. Of course, every writer will tell you—and they will believe it—that they are objective. But we have chosen what we think is important, and omitted details that we say don't matter. Is that objective? Is it a sort of lie by omission? No, it's the best we can do if we are honest.

So while I admit that I never got over the curious mixture of disdain (for Ali's womanizing and his cohorts) and astonishment, even admiration (I'm sure these feelings suffuse many reporters covering the president as well), I played another pivotal role in Ali's path to acceptance with officialdom in America.

He never should have gotten so far as to refuse to take the army pledge. He had flunked the army's entrance exam (after he did, he explained, "I only said I was the Greatest; I never said I was the smartest"). Others who failed this test simply were told to go home; they received a draft status that would keep them out of the service. The army didn't want people with low I.Q.s handling weapons, having buddies dependent on them.

Many people thought this was a facade, that Ali had purposely failed the test. After all, could a fellow who wrote poetry ("They all must fall/in the round I call") be so stupid as to fail an army entrance exam? But I had been a test administrator in the army, and I knew that unsophisticated people could have trouble with it—"Which bothers you more, sand or lightning?" was one question I myself had wrestled with. I had seen thousands of recruits come and go, taking this test. If you were decently educated, if you had a smidgen of reading experience, if you were part of the larger American society—well, you'd have no trouble with it. Ali, and who knows how many others like him, did not fall into these categories.

So I called his old high school principal in Louisville. I was curious to discover just what Ali's I.Q. was. But at this time in history, the I.Q. was coming under attack. It was race-biased, claimed some. It was class-biased, said others. The New York City school system, the nation's largest and often the leader in educational initiatives, had stopped talking about I.Q. It was an embarrassment. No one could find out anyone else's I.Q. This stance was evident across the rest of America as well. Schools had stopped discussing their students' scores.

I knew I would have to immediately ingratiate myself with the principal if I was to have any luck learning Ali's I.Q. number. I got through to the principal easily enough. I quickly told him I was trying to understand this whole phenomenon—an engaging, verbal fellow like Cassius Marcellus Clay (his younger brother was Rudolph Valentino Clay), unable to get even a passing grade on a test that had sent millions of Americans into uniform. I told him that my wife taught in New York City, and that she had run programs for gifted children, and wasn't always convinced that the brightest kids were identified properly. And then I added, "How many minority children do we miss, or saddle them with a failing number?"

The principal leaped at this.

"You're absolutely right," he said. "Look at Cassius Clay. He's got an I.Q. of 76. Now, what does that mean?"

Whew. When the man told me Ali's I.Q. number I felt like shouting "Eureka!" I had scored a scoop, and I had a story here that begged to be told. Imagine, an I.Q. of 76 for America's most famous test-taker— when the norm was 100.

Often, when we in the newspaper dodge interview people and uncover a nugget that we weren't supposed to know about, we keep talking quickly so the person at the other end doesn't realize what he has done or said. You don't want them to take it back. I remember Dustin Hoffman got this just right in *All the President's Men*, when he was interviewing a former secretary for the Committee to Reelect the President. When she told Hoffman/Carl Bernstein a damning bit of news, he gulped and then changed the subject, making some offhand remark about why he was taking out his notepad.

We don't get too many chances to do good works in the newspaper business. I was glad I got mine, showing that Ali legitimately did badly on tests and was not simply trying to avoid going into the military. And yet, for years afterward, I wondered how much help I inadvertently had given to the racist demagogues that surrounded Ali. Moments like this have made me accept the fact that we work in an imperfect business. Often, the whole truth as we know it cannot be shared because, quite simply, that's not the part of the story we're doing. In other words, some truth we write can obscure another truth.

I think about this when I recall my dinner with Mike Tyson at Don King's.

Las Vegas had become the capital of boxing by the 1990s, having long since displaced Madison Square Garden. The big hotels in Vegas found it profitable to invite the big spenders in for a heavyweight title fight, and so the fight camps stayed at the luxury hotels for free. It made sense, then, for King, who had become a boxing impresario (although one eventually sued by many of the fighters he promoted), to buy himself a place in Vegas.

Our paths first intersected in 1975. King had become prominent by ingratiating himself with the boxer of the day. He bragged, for example, that he had been Joe Frazier's promoter the night Frazier defended his heavyweight title against Foreman. After Foreman knocked out Frazier, King left the building with Foreman. King made an impression on everyone. His hair was brushed straight up, leading the columnist Red Smith to describe the coif as "hair by General Electric." King had a wonderfully quirky vocabulary—filled with polysyllabic words and words that he simply joined because they sounded right. One of my favorites was "trickeration," the art of fooling someone with sneakiness, which makes sense when you think about it.

King had a bone to pick with me. I had written a piece describing as absurd his claim that he had Arab oil-interest money ready to buy Madison Square Garden. That contention came about while he was negotiating to put on a title fight in the Garden, and King didn't like the offer he was getting from the Garden big shots. So why not threaten to buy the place from under them? I pointed out that in some of the places King had promoted fights, he left a trail of hapless investors who could never recoup their money (in fact, the country of Zaire had dropped ten million dollars on the famed Ali-Foreman "Rumble in the Jungle"). I also noted that Arab oil interests owning the Garden might not sit well with Knicks' season ticket-holders, most of whom were Jewish.

My phone rang the next day. It was King, calling me from England. He was going to be in New York the next day, and could he come to the *Times* to explain his position? Well, he came in, we met, sat around for an hour—and I enjoyed it. He told me of the difficulty he had in being taken seriously by the mainstream press, and that perhaps his criminal background was the reason. He told me how he spent all the time he could in the prison library while serving eight years for stomping to death a numbers runner in Cleveland who had held out on him. Reading, said King, made him realize there were other worlds out there besides being a street criminal.

Thus, he became enamored of words, and chewed them over and memorized the ones he really liked. I think he appreciated his day in court at the paper, and while I wasn't involved on a daily basis in boxing, we saw each other from time to time. Then, almost twenty years later, I took over the boxing beat for the *Times*. I did it for selfish reasons: Tyson was about to get out of jail, and King had been talking about promoting his fights in Asia and South America, even the Soviet Union. What a great way to wind down my career—as a world traveler. Also, in the newspaper business some of the best writing has been about boxing. It's such a simple sport that the writer is free to use all his adjectives, his clever phrases, his personal view of the action—with little worry that someone will disagree or edit him or her. After all, how can you argue with what I think I see?

So, ensconced as the boxing writer for the Paper of Record, I went to King's place a few nights before a Tyson fight. The idea was that a few of us, the beat writers for America's major papers, would have the chance to spend a relaxing evening with Tyson, perhaps get to see the other side of this guy who had just gotten out of prison for rape. Because boxing now had become driven by pay-per-view, instead of the live gate, promoters needed all the national (and international) publicity they could get. Every person who decided to watch the fight from home was going to pay $39.95.

I drove up to a gated community, where an off-duty Las Vegas policeman let me through. Then it was past more moonlighting cops, finally arriving at King's white mansion. I wondered how many of these police officers realized they were being paid to guard a guy who had served time for manslaughter.

Inside, it was décor by Kitsch. Most things were white—furniture, walls. We were ushered into an immense white living room, which had a wall the size of a theater movie screen. For good reason: at the press of a button, a screen came down from the ceiling to fill the wall.

Me with Don King, 1986.

After a while, Tyson came in and sat in a chair surrounded by five or six reporters. I sat next to my pal, Mike Katz of the *News*. He was the most noted boxing writer in the country. I had known Mike since the 1950s at City College of New York, and I always thought of him as the best newspaperman around. He could edit. He could write heads. He could write deft stories with an inviting lead and a wiseass sense of humor. Oh, a lot of the people he wrote about detested him. He had dubbed the golden boy of boxing, Oscar de la Hoya, "Chicken de la Hoya." De la Hoya's people tried to bar him from a news conference. Another world champion, Riddick Bowe, became "Ridiculous Bowe." And Mike would laugh in King's face when there was an obvious outrageous lie. But Mike was a good friend, very helpful, and a welcome companion in this strange new world of boxing.

My eyes took in the surreal scene: a relaxed Tyson, the white room. And, oh, yes. There was a white electronic Yamaha grand piano—it was playing Mozart! To my right, there was the kitchen, and I saw King in there eating from a box of Kentucky Fried Chicken, while Tyson was talking. Occasionally, King would wipe his fingers and leaf through a handy book of Goethe he liked to keep nearby. Mozart played on. Such serenity—outside, cops were making sure no one bothered the two former felons inside. It was one of the more delicious scenes of my working days.

Tyson was not so paranoid during moments like these, away from a stage where he often felt he was being grilled by prosecutors instead of reporters. Invariably, conversation always got around to how sinister outside forces were screwing him. This time, he was somewhat muted. He suggested that he had made enough money so that his children's children would never have to want anything again, which would be so different from his own childhood. We picked this up and spent a nostalgic hour talking about his childhood and his dreams, and he answered all our questions thoughtfully, even gladly, it seemed to me. Then he signaled it was over. One of his last statements was about his teenage petty crimes, and how he had been the child of a single mother. In other words, he had an explanation for why he had been a bad kid.

But by this time in my career, I did not have to defer to world-famous athletes. As a younger reporter I never would challenge outrageous statements. Few of us did. This time, though, Tyson had struck a nerve, for I was brought up a few blocks from where Tyson was—albeit many years earlier. And I was brought up by my mother, living in my grandparents' house. My parents had divorced when I was a year old.

"C'mon, Mike, cut the crap," I blurted suddenly. "I'm from East New York, too, and I was raised by a single mother. I didn't do any of the stuff you did." Tyson's response?

"You were! Did you know all those Jewish gangsters?"

I remembered then that Tyson, while in prison, had read about the old gangs of New York, and especially of those during the Depression days, when many were Jewish. This was before my time, though. Still, he seemed to get excited about my proximity to criminals.

"Well, I didn't really know them," I said. "But I had an uncle who was a bookmaker. He worked for some mob guys." Tyson wanted to know exactly where I had lived, and we spoke about the old neighborhood as if we had a bond, and a common understanding.

I'm not sure this little encounter changed my opinion of Tyson. But I believe it gave him new respect for me. I use the Tyson anecdote often in talking to journalism classes. For interviewing athletes is one of the most important parts of the job. It is an acquired skill.

3

Tricks of the Trade

No one at the paper taught you anything back in 1959. You were supposed to look clever, act clever, get the coffee order right. When you did all that, and showed you could write, they tossed you out into the field. No training program.

Still, I found it easy enough to connect to someone I was interviewing when it was, say, a high school coach. My address—the *New York Times*—preceded me. I already was ingratiated with that person.

But what about Joe Namath? Or Arnold Palmer? Or the suspicious Red Sox slugger Jim Rice? Or the crusty old Kentucky basketball coach, Adolph Rupp? How about the nutty Deion Sanders?

If you, the reader, were to come across Namath in a restaurant—I'm assuming you're not a sportswriter, too—I guarantee you'd want to talk to him. He transcended football. He made a movie with Ann-Margret, did a classic pantyhose commercial—all while he was playing. He had such wide media exposure that people thought they knew him. So most likely you might approach him and say something you thought was clever, or even smarmy, to break the ice. It happens all the time to athletes, every place they go. I have seen flight attendants ask Patrick Ewing for an autograph. I have seen the captain leave the cockpit to talk to Billy Martin. Everyone wants to get close to a celebrity.

Here's one very important thing about sportswriting—most of the time you're under deadline. You have to ask and talk and establish something between the two of you, and you have to do it while the athlete may feel shitty. He is tired, perhaps, or he has just lost, or he is in pain.

There is something else: Few of us are prepared to talk to celebrities we have read about, maybe even had looked up to from afar. What to say to Namath when I started covering the Jets in 1975? He had already done it all and seen it all. Namath's name was so ingrained in the American consciousness that one entrepreneur even started an employment agency called Mantle Men and Namath Girls—it was a job-search firm with he-man Mickey Mantle supposedly helping men find jobs while the sexy Namath found work for the women. It was a failed venture, but a window into America's perception of Namath. He was a living icon in helmet and pads, and he knew it. In fact, by 1975, six years after his guaranteed Super Bowl upset of the Colts, many years after he had stopped rebelling, he probably was voting Republican.

I was the new guy on the *Times* beat. The writer with the greatest impact had been the redoubtable Dave Anderson. In between, several other writers took over the Jets. Now it was my turn.

Here's what I knew about football: Glenn Davis and Doc Blanchard had played for West Point during World War II. I had heard of Doak Walker, the triple-threat hero of a heroic time. I knew about O. J. Simpson. I didn't watch football. I didn't know anything about the game. I did not know—and I am not kidding—what a tight end was.

But Anderson had given me advice when I told him I was taking over the Jets' beat: "When in doubt," he said, "write Namath." Of course, Dave had done that countless times. But it was easier for him because of a simple fact I was to learn later on: when you write about a superstar while they are young, before they have the great success, you are a part of their formative years in a way. You were there before the crowd was. Dave had been close to Joe before the Super Bowl. Joe's winning the Super Bowl punctuated their relationship, put the exclamation point on it.

Now to meet this famous person. Before a practice, Joe was standing on the sidelines. The simpler 1970s was a time when we could actually mingle with the players on the practice field at the Jets' camp. That was long before Bill Parcells took over and barred all but four people from watching practice—certainly, never the press. Parcells even kept his

Interviewing Joe Namath, 1976.

son-in-law, who was in charge of pro personnel, from viewing work-outs. But in those olden days, we writers—we even were allowed on the practice field with the players, behind the huddle.

"Watch out," someone would yell, "Joe's backpedaling." We made sure to move out of the way. I waited for a quiet moment, when the defense was on the field working out, and I sidled up to Joe as he spoke to a teammate.

"Joe, my name is Jerry Eskenazi," I told him. "I'm going to be covering the Jets for the *Times*—and I don't know anything about football."

He loved it.

"You know," he told me years later, "you were the only reporter who ever admitted to me he didn't understand football. I liked that." In fact, whenever he ran into me, following his retirement, he would love to tell that story to others. He tells it still.

The thing is, I was serious. I also had learned how to make contact with athletes in other ways. So when I found myself at Yankee Stadium, in that same era, when Reggie Jackson was reigning as the controversial star, and embroiled in constant arguments with the Boss, George Steinbrenner, and manager-for-now Billy Martin, I considered the ways to make Reggie notice me. Or at least pay attention to my questions. Reggie was full of himself, as perhaps would be most people who'd had a candy bar named after them and saw their picture on a box of Wheaties.

I had no luck the first few sentences, and finally, he simply walked away from me. Now I was truly challenged. What makes this man tick? I wondered. Then I remembered the famous quote about him. In base-ball-speak, a "hot dog" is a guy who shows off, who thinks a lot of himself. A teammate had once said of Jackson: "There isn't enough mustard in the world to cover that hot dog."

Reggie had an ego. But it was more than that, I thought. He also was a feeling individual whose stardom had kept him from being regarded with . . . what, compassion? All his manager, Martin, saw was a prima donna. All Steinbrenner saw was a guy making millions who didn't al-ways deliver (Reggie had not yet earned the sobriquet Mr. October). So I pushed myself back to Jackson, who regarded me with a polite stare. I might as well have been unloosing the flu on the room.

"You know, Reggie," I said. "I've always thought you were bigger than the people or teams you played for. I've always thought you had a sense of yourself that most people don't have. You understand who you are."

He nodded. Then he walked away, again. A minute later, someone tapped me on the shoulder. It was Jackson.

"I've been thinking about what you said. You're right. You want to have breakfast tomorrow?"

Ever have the feeling you have just aced a test, had come through something with flying colors, have done something that verifies your sense of yourself? At that moment, it was how I felt.

Namath, Reggie, DiMaggio—after that, it was easy. Although the great DiMag was suspicious, and you had to come at him with a smile and your hands out of your pockets.

Funny, though, it's been years since I had to concoct an introduction, to arm myself with something to say. Maybe I never had to in the first place. Maybe all I ever needed was a little confidence to know I could do it. Maybe that's all any of us—sportswriters, dentists, farmers, clean-up hitters—really need. Confidence.

There are ways to burnish that confidence, though, and many reporters, in and out of sports, never take the trouble to learn simple techniques. For example, if I'm meeting a player for the first time, I simply look in the press guide to find out something about his background. I am confident that there will be something in his history with which I can relate—either I'm familiar with his school, or hometown, or his major in college, or perhaps the job his mother or father held.

Sometimes, these aren't enough. One day my office asked me to talk to the Red Sox's silent slugger, Jim Rice—and not even about himself, but for a profile we were doing on his teammate, Fred Lynn. While the Red Sox were taking batting practice, one of the Boston writers asked me what I was doing. I told him I planned to interview Rice.

"Good luck," said the writer. "He doesn't talk to us."

Hmm. How to get this truculent hero to open up to me, a stranger? And from a rival city, to boot. Well, I did have a Jim Rice connection. Or rather my sons did, for I just had bought Mark and Mike a Jim Rice–model glove.

I went into the locker room after batting practice and approached Rice, who was taking off his shoes. I introduced myself. Not much reaction.

I made up a little white lie.

"Jim," I began, "I just bought my ten-year-old son a Jim Rice glove. It's stiff. I don't know how to break it in." His eyes lit up. He reached into his locker and asked, "which model is it?" and pulled out two gloves. I didn't realize there were two models. I pointed to one.

"Here's what you do," he went on, and then continued for five or six minutes as if he were giving the recipe for a complicated ratatouille. I made believe I was enthralled as he gave me pointers—"rub it with oil and tie it up"—and was genuinely interested to make sure I got it right. We were buddies. Then I hit him with my question. Dustin Hoffman couldn't have done it any better in his best Carl Bernstein imitation.

"By the way," I began, and told Rice my office wanted me to ask him about Lynn, the smooth-as-silk batter.

Without hesitation, Rice replied, "A picture out of *Vogue*."

How's that for a quote from a man's man? It was the lead to my story on Lynn.

I don't think I ingratiated myself quite so well with the infamous midget wrestler, Sky Lo-Lo. Unfortunately, I had a professional-wrestling problem. Vince McMahon, Sr., the impresario of modern pro wrestling, didn't like me. Once, I had written a story, tongue-in-cheek (and how else could you handle professional wrestling?) about his hefty marquee star, Bruno Sammartino. McMahon, whose son Vince was to take wrestling into the realm of pay-per-view and make it a mega-industry, was waiting for me one night as I entered the Garden.

"I don't like the stuff you've been writing," he growled. "What are you saying? It's fixed?" I shrugged. Well, of course, that was what I was saying. I didn't think anyone would notice. It's supposed to be fixed, isn't it? I thought.

This particular night featured the midgets. The bouts all ended the same way—the good guy is getting the crap beaten out of him. He is nearly dead. The bad guy climbs the ropes and is about to jump down at him. Suddenly, the good guy staggers to his feet and, just as the nasty guy is about to land, whacks him across the chin. Then the good guy somehow manages to fall atop the villain, the referee counts to three, and the match is over.

After Sky won his bout in this clichéd fashion, I took off for the locker room. Little did I know that the elder McMahon already had disrespected (a word that, infuriatingly, finds its way into my paper these days) me.

"Say, you guys have remarkable powers of recovery," I said to start the interview, hoping to ingratiate myself with the little fellow. "What do you mean?" said Sky Lo-Lo without smiling. Then he walked up to me, looked up, and said, "What are you trying to say—it's fixed?"

Well, this was one of those rare moments that came as an integrity check. I blew it.

"No, of course not," I sort of stammered. "I mean, you're in good shape." I don't think Sky bought it, but he said, "Yeah," grudgingly, and added, "whaddya wanna know?"

I escaped from the locker room, which he shared with the guy he had just beaten, as quickly as possible. I had lost my integrity, but was still intact.

Not quite as menacing but just as suspicious, Rickey Henderson tried my patience. But I persevered. The greatest base-stealer of all time (as he once described himself, quite accurately) was another of those athletes who squinted their eyes when I approached them.

I could tell he wasn't in a talkative mood. So I said, "Just want to let you know that forty years ago I got Jackie Robinson's autograph when he was baseball's best base-stealer." I got little reaction from Rickey. I slogged on, though. I told Henderson I then asked Robinson, "How come you're not stealing so many bases this year, Jackie?" Henderson seemed interested.

"What did he say?" Henderson asked me.

"Robinson told me, 'You've got to get on base first, kid.'"

Henderson laughed at the story. I had connected. He understood on several levels what Robinson meant.

"That's true," Henderson said. "You can't steal second base from home plate."

And yet, while I admit I have resorted to trickeration to get stories such as this, there have been moments when the event simply told itself, and I needed only to be an observer who got it right. Those are the times when being a sportswriter makes you really feel you have gotten lucky, and that while your best friends from the old neighborhood are making more money, you're the one with the fun job—even, I might say, an important job. Still, I wasn't always aware of how important an event was at that moment, when I was caught up with catching a plane, or making a deadline, or being able to write while wearing gloves in an Alpine winter, say.

Case in point: It was a long drive from my place in Forest Hills, Queens, where my wife and I were living in 1965, to Princeton, New Jersey. My job: to write about Princeton's basketball team, an Ivy League school going to the NCAA semi-finals. This didn't happen much any more. I was, I have to admit, slightly bored by the prospect of the story. Also, inconvenienced. You can't get to Princeton easily from anywhere, and at the end you wind up on a two-lane road and you spend too much time driving.

But it wasn't only the trip that annoyed me. I was, with the self-righteousness of someone who had gone to a college that cost about forty dollars a year (and what a stink we made when they wanted to increase the student-activity dues), cynical of the Ivy League. Ah, I had often thought, if I had been a legacy, I probably would have waltzed into Columbia. Yet as I chugged along in my gulf-blue 1962 Volkswagen, I imagined what it must be like to have attended a school like Princeton.

Naturally, I had believed my alma mater, CCNY, was America's best college. The kids that went there, I figured, didn't have parents who knew bankers who could get them into the Ivies. And certainly we didn't know congressmen to nominate us for West Point. So what happened at other colleges, on the basketball courts or gridiron, really wasn't important, and probably my classmates felt the same way. You couldn't get into City College merely because you stood 6 feet 7 inches tall, or because you could carry a football. Indeed, big-time sports had become almost loathsome at my school. It had been just a few years earlier that the basketball scandals had rocked America, and City College of New York had been at the hub. There was something even more insidious about those scandals, in which City, while going on to capture the NCAA and NIT titles, had been shaving points.

What was unspoken in the scandals, and afterwards, was that virtually all the players at City were black or Jewish. Their Grand Slam had been a victory for diversity (before the term had its present connotation). It was a victory for an urban consciousness, for the American dream, for whatever myths we held about New York City. And then when the scandals erupted, whatever myths the rest of the country held about us seemed to actually come true.

Thus, at City we didn't play basketball at the Garden any longer. Our big sports were soccer and lacrosse. In fact, while I was at the school, we won the NCAA soccer title with a goalie born in Italy and a star striker from Hungary who had barely escaped the Soviet invasion of his country. It was a different sort of melting-pot team, but the only people who really cared were us—the students.

So being a big-time athlete had ceased to be important at City College of New York. Size and strength hardly mattered any more—if you wanted to be a soccer or lacrosse player, or a fencer. These didn't help you get into the school. What counted was the average. You either had a high enough high school average to get in, or you took an admissions test that, combined with the high school grade, had to be fairly high. There were no mitigating circumstances—not being a legacy, not money, not the ability to play the bassoon or carry a football. This created an elitist culture among us Beavers—how's that for a school nickname for an industrious community of scholars?—who knew, just knew, that at the big-time athletic schools the rules were bent.

Thus, I never was in awe of most of the athletes I covered. Bill Bradley? Well, perhaps this guy was different. But he also was tall and that made him suspect. Would Princeton have taken him if he were 5-6 instead?

So with some indifference, I saw this rather gangly looking fellow standing on top of a bus at Princeton as the school was having a ball bidding its basketball team good-bye on the way to the Final Four. As I recall, he was wearing a jacket, and had a scarf draped around his neck. A very large Holden Caulfield, I thought. He was leading the cheers.

Some years later, after he had forestalled his professional basketball career to study at Oxford, I happened to cover his first pro game as a New York Knick. He had just arrived from his stint as a Rhodes Scholar. I saw the back of a very big man watching from the sidelines. Unmistakably, it was Wilt Chamberlain. I asked him, "Wilt, what will this be like for him?"

Wilt was affable. He patted me on the rump, said, "Hiya, Jerry," as if he knew me.

"He's going to have to handle the pressure," said the world's most famous basketball player. "He's going to have to get used to people having high expectations for him every game he plays." Wilt knew.

The next time I came across Bill Bradley was almost thirty years later, at LaGuardia Airport. He was a U.S. senator and was making a run for the presidency. He knew my name, and we had a terrific talk about sports and government. After our chat, I changed my mind about Princeton.

Bill Bradley standing on a bus. Who knew that he'd be a senator and have designs on the White House? But it points up a fact for those of us in the business for a long time—today's story can be tomorrow's legend. Often, you don't know at that moment, for you're simply interested in getting the information and writing the story before deadline, and getting home.

It's not easy to know when you have a historic story—or one that could prove historic. Yet, there are events that even jaded newspaper reporters understand are significant, and will change forever the way we write about them.

The first Ali-Frazier clash, at Madison Square Garden, certainly was that. My assignment for that 1971 event was to write about scalping and how people got their hands on tickets. There was something outrageous about that bout. The Garden was charging one hundred dollars for ringside seats, a high-water figure that seemed beyond the pockets of even big-spending fight-goers. Why, Broadway orchestra seats hadn't even hit a fifty-dollar top. A one-hundred-dollar charge for a seat was as outrageous as, say, a million-dollar-a-year salary for a baseball player.

But there was something else brewing in this bout. There are sports events, and then there are mega-events. This was going to take sports— and, in a way, show business—into a new era. It was sport as theater, and it was about money and celebrity and power. It was a foreshadowing of rock concerts, of Grammy awards, of blockbuster sports events. Yes, there was the intrigue and the drama of the two fighters. And there was that outrageous amount of money being charged. There was tens of millions of dollars more to be made from pay-per-view screenings around the world.

As I swarmed around the Garden the day of the bout, I saw tickets changing hands for a thousand dollars. A Garden vice president told me he had been offered a package deal of ten thousand dollars for his five seats. I saw "players," grandly dressed pimps and their ladies swooping into the Garden, like royalty. There was such a crush of reporters and television people that each of us was given a baseball-type cap to wear to distinguish us from someone who might have had a phony ticket. The ringside scene had established a new tone for these spectaculars.

Consider this: Frank Sinatra was leaning on the ring apron taking photographs for *Life*. Burt Lancaster was doing the pay-per-view television analysis. Colonel Sanders, the Kentucky Fried Chicken founder, was wearing his white suit and ensconced in a ringside seat.

The next day, my scalping story—not the fight story—was the lead of the *Arizona Republic*: a big, black headline ran across the top of the front page with the words "$1,000 a ticket."

Of course, had I known then how this would be a turning point in American sports, and show business, I might have said so. But I didn't know. Neither of those arbiters of the famous, Joan Rivers and her daughter, Melissa, was there to interview the stars. As a reporter, you get so caught up in the noise and the lights and the minutiae of the moment—you are bombarded by nineteen thousand voices and hundreds of lights and the clatter of the motorized cameras—that you try your best to capture the immediacy of the scene in front of you.

4

Dealing with Icons

Donald Trump wanted to buy a football team in the mid-1980s. And once he did (the New York Generals of the United States Football League), he wanted to buy a player—actually, to own a player. What better symbol of being the master of his domain—all of New York—than owning New York's greatest athlete? Thus, Donald Trump bought and owned Lawrence Taylor, the magnificent, troubled star of the football Giants.

The Donald always had this basic idea of the sports business: if you have more money, you buy a better team. Makes sense. Of course, none of the other owners in this league that hoped to be a less costly springtime version of the NFL had his money. They wanted to put a cap on spending. He wanted to spend whatever it took. That made perfect sense to him. When he spoke of owning things, he used the metaphor of "owning a place on Fifth Avenue instead of Columbus Avenue."

One day I treated Trump to lunch at the paper. We have several private dining rooms where *Times* bigwigs take visiting heads of state, and, once in a while, sportswriters buy billionaires a meal. I think Trump trusted me, and he also was interested in what I knew. I had been covering the Jets and the NFL for ten years, and I understood about unions, and television contracts, and team organization.

It was a good symbiotic relationship because, let's face it, I was interested in Trump and what made him tick. He had become New York's—

and possibly the country's—most noted real-estate mogul. The fact that he now was in the sports business made him a person I needed to write about. Luckily for me, he had read my stuff, or at least he claimed he had.

I wanted to know his plans to get Taylor, who had become football's biggest star. Taylor redefined how defenses attack, he had been voted the league's top defensive player as a rookie, he hurt people. He had also shown the wild side that he used to demonstrate at the University of North Carolina, where he famously had climbed the side of a frat building. Now a full-fledged star, Taylor was getting miffed. The contract he had signed as a Giants' rookie was coming to an end, and he wanted a heck of a lot more to renew it. If not, he would be a free agent. So Trump gave him a million dollars—in cash—to jump teams. The money was a binder for a personal-services contract in which Taylor would make the leap to Trump's Generals.

Trump called me one day. I could hear him licking his lips as he spoke of having the vaunted National Football League on the run, and he relished the ownership of Lawrence Taylor. Every day, said Trump, Taylor would call his bank and ask about the million dollars, which was deposited in a money-market account earning 7 percent interest. Each day, $191.78 would be posted to the account. That was almost $1,400 a week, almost $6,000 a month. And Taylor, who by now also was in financial difficulties, would have that $70,000 a year, maybe even for the rest of his life.

Imagine the sight of this huge, violent man looking at his money market account daily, that $191.78 accruing, stretching into infinity.

What if, I asked Trump, the Generals failed. What would you do with Taylor and his personal-services contract then?

"I'd put him in a doorman's uniform and have him work at one of my buildings," Trump replied.

Now, The Donald hardly was a typical owner—but in a way he was part of the new breed of owners that had taken over sports teams in the 1980s, and since. They bought them, rather than inherited or built them.

The Wrigleys were planning to put lights in their great old park; Tom

Yawkey was on his last legs in Boston; names such as Crosley and Comiskey had faded from baseball. Beer companies owned hockey teams. Corporations began to own Madison Square Garden, going from Roosevelt Raceway to I.T.T. to even bigger fry. There were a few remaining football owners of another era: Wellington Mara and Art Rooney, and even Art Modell had become iconic, although his beginnings in money-making had been on Madison Avenue.

Because these new mega-millionaires had bought the teams after making fortunes in other fields, they had come to think of their clubs as a commodity much like their other lines of business. Trump was part of a group of men who were usually wildly successful, but whose ranks included the buccaneering sorts—the art collector/businessman from Canada, Peter Pocklington, who owned the Edmonton Oilers; or Bruce McNall, who collected antiquities and coins and owned the Lakers and Kings. He brought Wayne Gretzky to the United States but his suspect businesses sent him into bankruptcy and prison.

Some of these fellows made bizarre promises to entice stars to jump to their clubs. I remember talking to Clarence Campbell, the courtly president of the National Hockey League for a quarter of a century, the day that free-agency became a fact of life in baseball.

"It will change sports in ways you cannot imagine now," he told me in 1974.

Indeed, it has. When my love of sports was shaped growing up in Brooklyn, in the late 1940s and 1950s, the same players were on the same team year after year, virtually throughout my teens. To this day I can tell you their numbers and names—Hodges on first, Jackie on second, Pee Wee at short, Cox at third, Campy catching—and so on. These guys were mythic, yet so close. They were a subway ride away. Or, as the fifties dawned, you could catch them on television every home game, as well as the eleven games a year they played at the Polo Grounds. One golden day, up at Coogan's Bluff, I got the autographs of Gil Hodges, Jackie Robinson, Roy Campanella, Duke Snider. All had neat, readable signatures.

Many years later, I was in the Yankees' dugout schmoozing with Bobby Murcer, their popular outfielder. A kid thrust a chewing-gum baseball card in front of him to sign.

**Clarence Campbell,
National Hockey League
commissioner.**

"I'm sorry," Murcer told the youngster. "I don't do cards." When I asked Murcer why, he replied, "The kids sell them. I never see a dime of it."

It has always amazed me that some of the most prominent people in the world—not merely in the world of sports—love seeing their names in the paper. Count among those, to my surprise, Chuck Yeager, the folksy hero of *The Right Stuff*—the first pilot to break the sound barrier.

The possibility of stories is endless—especially when you have a cooperative subject. I had tried to approach journalism in offbeat ways. Sure, you can interview a person in an office or in a media setting. But you get a very different type of story if you can do it in that person's haunts.

In 1988 I was covering the Indianapolis 500 (for a stretch I was the paper's auto-racing writer). That year, Chuck was the driver of the pace car, and I thought, what a great idea for a story—go for a spin in the pace car with the man who had been the world's fastest human.

This was really the second time I had the idea for this sort of piece.

Many years before a fellow named Craig Breedlove, who broke the land speed record in a rocket-powered vehicle at the Bonneville Salt Flats in Utah, came to New York on a publicity tour for a tire company. Why not go for a spin in Manhattan with the world's fastest driver, I thought? This we did. I think it was a Buick. We were parked on Seventh Avenue and he pulled out—without signaling, and almost was clipped by a passing car. We went about a block or two and he remarked on the traffic and how people weaved in and out erratically. Then we came to a red light. Breedlove calmly made a right turn, and it seemed all the horns in New York were turned on him. "What's wrong?" he said. "You can't make a turn on red in New York City," I explained.

I got my story.

Now, I was enjoying meeting General Chuck Yeager, sixty-five years old. I told him my idea—tooling around the track in the Oldsmobile Cutlass Supreme pace car. He at the wheel; me recording his comments. Boy, did he take to it. He invited me along on a practice run.

We strapped ourselves in, and the next thing I knew I was feeling G-forces. He took off like a teenager in a drag race on a country road.

"How do you like that?" he chortled. "In the race I'll 'cob' it. That's fighter-pilot talk to hit it." He explained he would hit 140 miles an hour before peeling off and letting the cars behind him charge into the race.

As we approached Turn 3, he said, "Up ahead are three signs. I can see them. You can't. I've got extraordinary eyesight." It wasn't a boast. It was a fact. I was glad he did, at the speed we were going.

Now we approached the pit area and he pressed hard on the brakes and he spoke again about the G-forces as we slammed to a stop. For the moment, he was back in his X-airplane, breaking the sound barrier, or perhaps re-creating the dog flights over Europe, where he shot down thirteen enemy fighters—including five on one afternoon—more than forty years earlier.

"I've got 20-10 eyesight from 8 inches out," he said. "I see things few people do."

The next day we came across each other in the pit area. Yeager was grinning broadly. I thought he was probably happy about the approaching race. He turned to a friend and called me over to introduce us.

"See this guy," he said to the friend. "He's the one that wrote about me

Chuck Yeager. IMS Photo.

in the *New York Times* today." Yeager sounded as if he had accomplished something.

On the other hand, Yankees' commander-in-chief George Steinbrenner was alternately attracted to, and repelled by, the press. Certainly, there was one instance when I repelled him.

It was my first experience at baseball spring training, the fantasy assignment for every sportswriter. As a kid, I used to read about those five weeks under the Florida sun, pitchers and catchers loosening up, Grapefruit League games, writers even taking batting practice, days at a motel pool. What could be a greater fantasy to a youngster in snowbound Brooklyn? Or, for that matter, to a grown-up who believes that journalism is a calling and that sportswriting is its bonus?

Well, spring training was and wasn't all it's cracked up to be. When you're around the Yankees and Steinbrenner, it's always something. And once again, the issue of what is fit to write about came up.

Steinbrenner is an engaging fellow, when he wants to be. He also can be nasty and surly (just ask the people in his office, including one secretary who mistakenly got him a tuna fish salad sandwich instead of chicken; she wound up crying after he screamed at her). We were standing in front of the first base seats during an exhibition game against the Pirates. The umpire at first base was from the National League. George was being very interesting in our conversation about baseball and life—this, after all, was during a leisurely, sunny March day when spring training is the most perfect setting in America for a sports fan—when a Yankee hit a ground ball to short.

Steinbrenner stopped talking as he watched the play unfold. The runner hustled to first, the shortstop threw—and the ump called an out.

"You fucking homer!" shouted Steinbrenner at the ump.

What startled me was not the word. What was so gross about that moment was that Steinbrenner was standing a few feet from the fans, and had no qualms about the invective. Nor did he seem concerned that he also was next to me, a newspaper reporter, or that the umpire and the players could hear him. It hardly mattered to the Boss, as he is known, that this was an exhibition game that counted for nothing. It didn't matter to him that he offended, even startled, fans and children within earshot. That tiny event said reams about Steinbrenner and his ways, and it disgusted me.

Sure, I had heard all the stories—and they were true—about his good works, about how he had furnished scholarships for poor kids, had loaned money to needy employees, had routinely given to charity. And then there was the despicable side of him—the side that could make a secretary cry, or a fan cringe.

Of course, the f-word didn't make its way into my story. But Steinbrenner's whining did. The head of the umpires' union, Richie Phillips, called me. I had a quandary. I didn't write the specifics of what the Boss had said. On the other hand, what he did say was virtually public record—shouted out in a stadium. Was I telling tales out of school to ask Phillips if he planned any formal complaint against George? Again, in my mind was this: what is my role as a reporter? Was I promoting a story for my own ends?

I muse, at times like these, over a famous, and controversial, statement made by the author Janet Malcolm in the *New Yorker*.

"Every journalist who is not too stupid or too full of himself to notice what is going on knows what he does is morally indefensible," she began. Her point was that we are all dishonest, using bits and pieces that serve us—discarding other items that could contain truths but that don't further our own agenda. She described us as "preying on people's vanities . . . gaining their trust and betraying them."

Well, that could be true for some victims. On the other hand, I figured that George Steinbrenner was a big boy. I told Phillips what Steinbrenner had shouted out in his moment of anger. Phillips was outraged.

The next thing I knew, Steinbrenner phoned me. Now, George didn't know me and I didn't know him, other than any relationship we may have had in three or four interviews over the years. I wasn't the Yankees' beat writer, and I certainly had never met Steinbrenner in a social setting. Our interaction had been strictly professional. George was very upset with what I had told Phillips, who was murmuring about making a formal complaint to the commissioner's office.

"Jerry, if you continue this it will go badly with our friendship," Steinbrenner said. It was the first time I realized George Steinbrenner and I were friends.

I did not back down, however.

"Wait a second, George," I said. "You didn't tell me this in confidence. You yelled 'Fucking homer!' at a ballpark. I don't see anything wrong with repeating what you said in public." I was, quite honestly, surprised by my own bravado. Had I gone too far?

"Well, maybe you're right," Steinbrenner said.

We said good-bye quite cheerily, I thought. Maybe it was because I had stood up to him? Maybe it was because I really felt good about saying the truth—even though Janet Malcolm may believe I had been naughty.

Sometimes it feels good to slap around a bully. Or at least embarrass him.

I am speaking to Joe DiMaggio for the first time in my life. It is the mid-1960s, many years after he retired. He is back for one of those old-timers' days. I have been a reporter for only a few years. We are sitting in the press room at Yankee Stadium, which really is more like a club. Old writers, old ballplayers, old managers stroll in, drinking at the bar. Di-Maggio, and everyone else, is smoking. Until this moment, I had seen him only on black-and-white television and in newsreels.

I wish I had been in this room when I was sixteen years old, instead of now, as an adult, trying to feel professional and not like a fan. The child may be father of the man, but when you're working, you're not a kid any longer. So I put away my childish toys, put away the veneration, the pure awe of being so close to a legendary ballplayer, and instead adopted the persona of the professional. I was a sportswriter.

How I had longed for this moment when I was writing high school sports for the *Liberty Bell* newspaper at Thomas Jefferson High School in Brooklyn. How I had daydreamed about this while taking the one journalism class offered at CCNY. How I had imagined how I would write it when I read the *Daily News* or the *New York Post* on the A train taking me up to 125th Street and my daily trek to City College. But now it is dinnertime, and I am introduced to Joltin' Joe. Very pleasant man. He is telling a story about an at-bat against Bob Feller back when he was a player.

"I didn't know what he was going to throw me," DiMaggio says. "That must have made you uncomfortable," I say, trying to connect, to show empathy.

DiMaggio stops, and stares at me.

"Now you're prying," he says. And stops chewing. He is glum. What is the matter with me? I think. I'm meeting the great DiMag and I screw up?

"No," I protested weakly. "I was just saying how I would feel. I wasn't prying. If it seemed like that, I'm sorry."

"OK," he says. It is OK. I am not on his shit list. He continues talking. The air comes back into the room.

I learned something in that moment—besides the epiphany that you should never meet your heroes. Even the greatest want something of themselves kept from view—but they also want you to know about them.

DiMaggio wasn't the only remarkable sports figure who misinterpreted my intentions. More shocking to me than Joltin' Joe's suspicious nature was that none other than Howard Cosell, whom I believe was the

finest combination of journalist and broadcaster, had a hissy fit over
something I wrote. And yet, it was written in private.

Cosell was, of course, known for his signature phrase "I'm telling it
like it is." He would scold icons of all stripes, even his friends, if he thought
they were not doing the right thing. Essentially, Howard was more famous for being churlish than he was for being an advocate of liberal
causes and journalistic integrity. What surprised me most about him,
though, was his thin skin.

First, let me say that Howard was one of the most gracious and gen-
erous people (when he wanted to be). I was a guest on his radio show,
plugging a book I had written on the football Giants' glory days. Unlike
most interviewers with whom I had gone on the air, Cosell actually read
my book. He asked serious questions and was kind in his praise—he
even complimented me on it during a *Monday Night Football* television
broadcast. After the radio interview, we went to the famous Midtown
restaurant Twenty-One, and Cosell said to me, in a loud voice as we
were entering, "Watch how many people come over to me. I've got one
of the highest recognition factors in America. I'm on the list of both
most admired and most detested people."

Some time later, during a trip to Houston, I picked up the *Chronicle*
and noticed an ad at the bottom of one of the sports pages. Fans of the
Oilers were upset because the team had not been on *Monday Night*

**Howard Cosell, with Joe Namath.
Photo courtesy of ABC Sports.**

Football for years. The reason was quite simple: the Monday night games are the league's showcase, and the schedule-makers attempt to put together two teams they believe are in the elite sector. The Oilers had been a losing team for a long time. Of course, Howard got blamed for the ABC snub. So some enterprising person put an ad in the *Houston Chronicle* that offered "Go to Hell Cosell" T-shirts for ten dollars apiece. Amused, I clipped the ad and mailed it to Howard at his ABC office. I enclosed a note that read, "Can I get the New York franchise for these shirts?" As usual, he was working a Monday night game the following week. In those cushy days, the network often would fly the broadcasters back to New York by private jet when the games ended. So Cosell probably got home at four or five in the morning on Tuesday.

But at 8 A.M. my phone rang.

"This is Howard Cosell," he announced.

Before I could even exchange a "Good morning," he launched into a tirade.

"Jerry Eskenazi. How could you? After all I've done for you."

I asked him what he was talking about.

"Don't you know my secretary opens my mail?" he said. "How could you embarrass me like that by sending me that thing from the Houston newspaper?"

I was, to say the least, incredulous. He must have waited all night to phone me. Was he serious? Television's great attack dog whimpering over a practical joke?

I realized he was serious, indeed, almost distraught.

"Howard," I said, in a soothing voice, "it was just a joke. You know how much respect I have for you."

"Oh," he said.

We said good-bye, both of us feeling better.

5

The Women

Jackie Robinson broke the color barrier in baseball when I was just eleven years old. But the Civil Rights movement in sports that I got to observe and write about was for women.

Sometimes, it takes thirty years to realize where you were at a moment in time that has significance today. And that you don't look at things quite the same way now as you did then.

This moment—one of many, it seems, that increasingly alter my viewpoint as the years go by—came in 2002. It was the thirtieth anniversary of the date when women for the first time were allowed to run side-by-side with men—even though they were not officially recognized as coequals—in the New York City Marathon. Indeed, it may have been one of the first times in a major American sport that this mixing of the sexes occurred.

I was there when it happened, writing it for the *Times,* and as I look at the yellowed clipping of the race, I am struck by its flippant tone. Then again, I guess you had to be there.

If you think of the marathon as it has come to be known—the majestic start on the Verrazzano Bridge, the snake dance through all the five boroughs, the eerie sight of the runners pounding over the 59th Street Bridge into Long Island City—well, it was a simpler time back then. The New York City Marathon of 1972 did not even encompass all of New York City, just Manhattan. The route was only a few miles long, from Central Park south, then north to 110th Street—back and forth, four times, to complete the 26 miles 385 yards.

In the intervening years, it has become a world event with thirty thousand runners, encompassing all of the city. About ten thousand of the competitors now are women. But back in 1972, a grand total of six women were in the race. The Amateur Athletic Union (the sport's governing body) decreed they had to start separately from the 272 men.

It had been only a few years since the Boston Marathon's men-only code was breached by the notorious "K. Switzer"—Kathy Switzer, who had entered using her first-name initial, allowing herself to slip past the entrance requirements. When the meet director, the middle-aged Jock Semple, saw her in the race, he ran out in his street clothes and attempted to rip the number off her shirt, but was elbowed aside by another runner. Switzer finished the race.

But now, on this fall day in Central Park in 1972, the genie was out, for the ferment of the women's movements—protesting everything from bras to abortions to equal pay—was in full swing. Thus, the six hardy women who showed up for the grinding event refused to run by themselves when the starter's gun for the women's segment went off— ten minutes before the men were scheduled to begin. The A.A.U. rules then forbade women from competing with the men. So the women had been directed to start separately. This fine fall day, though, the women were not having a separate-but-equal race. One of the women held a sign that read "Hey AAU Wake Up—It's 1972." Another sign read, in what I like to think was not a misspelling but a wry comment, "The AAU Is Midevil."

So when the gun went off—and someone in the crowd screamed "Right on!"—the women sat at the starting point in Central Park. The cry of "Right on!" was a sort of Civil Rights urging to tell it—in this case, sit it—like it is. They sat for ten minutes and refused to budge.

As the judges milled about frantically deciding what to do with the Central Park Six, a woman's voice in the crowd railed, "Chauvinist pig!" Fred Lebow, the bearded guru of New York racing, came over to me and whispered he would allow the women to run with the men if they'd stop this protest business, but he would never tell the A.A.U. that.

"Theoretically, they're not running with the men," he explained. So the gun went off proclaiming the "men's race." That is when the women finally stood up and joined the fray and—yes—ran with the men!

When it was over, some three hours later, all the women's times were announced as ten minutes slower than they actually ran—since they had not been allowed to start with the men. It reminded me that the Constitution had once decreed slaves' votes as being worth three-fifths of a white man's.

In my story, I described the fastest woman, Nina Kuscsik, as "a mother of three from Huntington, Long Island." Nothing further about her— no athleticism, no further insight. No quotes. Really, my story was about a bunch of people trying to figure out what to do. The protest took up more space than the running—indeed, I did not even use an adjective to describe the race. However, maybe I was on to something after all. While I thought at the time it was all an amusing distraction, perhaps another part of me understood that this was a sea change in sports. Soon, we'd have Billie Jean King playing against Bobby Riggs; we'd have Martina Navratilova slamming the ball and rushing the net; we'd have Jackie Joyner-Kersee, muscles rippling, running into history.

Of course, way back then, most of the stories we wrote about women in sports focused as much on aspects of their femininity as on what they accomplished, and we defined them as being single or married.

In 1973, Billie Jean King was going to play tennis against Bobby Riggs, once one of the best players in the world, but now a hustler, a vagabond character. He once used a broom instead of a racquet to beat an opponent—for money, of course. I was asked to cover the press conference, billed as Man vs. Woman, in the Astrodome, in this post-Freudian, neo-Friedan world. What I discovered at the conference was a liberation army of tough-talking women, their speech littered with words like "fuck" and "shit," in sharp contrast to Mrs. King (she was married to her promoter), who was gracious and serious. Oh, maybe she had a bit of a smile at times. But the other women there—I swear I felt my scrotum shrinking. It was the most outrageous locker-room language I had ever heard. In fact, you don't hear a lot of that language around male athletes—more, actually, from the coaches.

Riggs reveled in the man versus woman thing. He kept referring to Billie Jean as a "broad" and "girl" and dismissed her chances. But there was an air of butchiness rather than bitchiness surrounding the announcement. One of our reporters, Grace Lichtenstein, who made a point when speaking to men of peppering her conversations with various combinations of the f-word, went up to Riggs and asked him if his hair was real. Riggs, who had some kind of orange-colored, dyed weave, claimed it was.

"Can I pull it?" she asked. It was more of a dare than a question. Riggs consented. It was the first time in sports I had been around athletics used as a political rally, in which womankind was showing its balls. I thought the loudness and vulgarity of it was absurd. But there is a thesis, antithesis, and synthesis in every major social movement, and so there was in women's sports. I've got to confess, though, that the antithesis stayed with me for quite a while.

In those tumultuous times, there was so much that was being redefined about sportswriting as well. I had to adjust. Yes, I'm from another time, when, for example, women didn't say "fuck." At least not for publication. But I was present at the creation of the mainstream women's sports movement in three major areas, and I believe my reporting had something to do with moving things along—both for the female athletes, and for the female sportswriters.

It was disingenuous to suggest, for example, that women reporters be allowed the same locker-room privileges as their male colleagues. Everyone knew that men don't go into women's locker rooms—I'm sure that neither Martina nor Billie Jean nor golfer Mickey Wright would have permitted that. Yet there was this growing belief that there were no barriers between the sexes, no differences, in fact, and that since everyone was created equal (or at least held a press pass), a woman reporter should have the same ability as a male reporter to interview a player while he was scratching his balls.

This dichotomy—I wasn't allowed in a woman's locker room, but they could enter a man's—symbolized the hard-and-fast stance that I felt was being taken by an increasingly raucous women's movement.

And then a human face was put on it for me.

Just a few months later, my wife and I were driving up to Kitchener, Ontario, for the opening of the Rangers' hockey training camp. My sports editor, a truly kind man from Queens named James Roach, had just hired a reporter named Robin Herman—the first full-time woman sportswriter at the paper. She also was a member of Princeton's first women's graduating class. Robin was going to learn to be a hockey writer, and I was going to tutor her. She accompanied us on the drive up.

Robin was smart, very professional. I suppose I looked for "feminine" moments from her—something that would indicate a woman's approach to the game, as opposed to a professional (that is to say, male) outlook. I was surprised when this didn't happen. For like most men my age—indeed, most people my age—I had thought of the world of sports as a male domain. After all, on street corners in Brooklyn, when we discussed batting averages, or made trades between the Yankees and Dodgers, we were in the company of males. I don't think I had ever discussed Jackie Robinson or Johnny Lujack with a girl. The only women I had come across in the sports business in the 1960s and the dawn of the 1970s—in addition to the athletes—were secretaries. Certainly, women had no presence in television or radio sports, either.

The morning after we arrived in Canada, Robin came down to breakfast with us, shaken. A player had asked her to do the interview in his room. She went up there, fought him off, and emerged without a story, but intact.

My wife, Roz, spoke to Robin about being smart, about understanding that she was going to be seen as a woman first—and that athletes had little sophistication to separate the woman from the reporter. Robin was a piece of meat to some athletes.

Robin eventually became the Rangers' beat writer and was one of the first—if not the first—women sports reporters for a major American newspaper. But when she interviewed players, she was not allowed in the dressing room. In my role as president of the newly formed hockey writers association, I insisted that she be given full equal privileges, and not simply separate-but-equal status. I knew, of course, that she was placed at a disadvantage by interviewing players in a hallway. Players were being summoned to speak, instead of simply hanging out at their locker, engaging in informal banter, surrounded by their teammates. With Robin, though, they were being interviewed in a damned hallway. She prevailed and made a name for herself in the business. We lost contact. The last I heard she had written a book about a nuclear reactor at Princeton.

But her impact on sportswriting was palpable. Eventually, the Islanders, and then the Rangers, and then other hockey teams relented, and women entered the steamy, noisy world of the men's locker room. Other sports were brought, kicking and screaming, into this new phenomenon of women reporters. The Dallas Cowboys, who always prided themselves on class, passed out spiffy bathrobes to its players to wear while being interviewed.

Still, I'll always remember the sight of the *Daily News*'s Lawrie Mifflin, a dogged reporter who was unflappable, interviewing the Rangers' biggest player, Phil Esposito, as he stood wearing only a towel, but with one leg raised on a wooden bench. God bless her.

A few years later I was teaching journalism at Adelphi University on Long Island. I brought the class to a hockey game and of course to the locker room afterwards. After all, I was immersing my students in the gestalt experience of journalism. By then, players were accustomed to women in the room, and many of the players simply walked around naked. Robin had opened the door, so to speak, for the women that followed.

When I recounted the locker-room scene to my wife, telling her about the naked players and my students, some of whom were teenage girls, she told me sweetly, "You're going to get arrested by the girls' parents." I thought that was funny. But you know, some part of me wondered: what if I were the father of a nineteen-year-old girl whose professor took her to a room filled with naked men?

The official, federal stamp soon was placed on women as equal-opportunity competitors by Title IX. Essentially, it demanded that America's sixteen thousand public-school systems and twenty-seven hundred colleges and graduate schools grant equal opportunity to women or suffer a loss in federal funds.

I went to Washington, D.C., in 1973 to write that story. It turned out to be one of the most complex, and misunderstood, regulations that anyone, in or out of sports, had dealt with. I sensed this from my first moments after talking to Secretary of Health, Education and Welfare Caspar Weinberger, and then officials of major colleges. They were at odds, and Weinberger's successors and college officials remain at odds. The athletic director at the University of Michigan, for example, predicted intercollegiate athletics "would simply collapse" if a liberal interpretation was made of the guidelines. The NCAA charged that funds would instead be funneled into non-money-making sports such as women's basketball or women's track and field. "I don't think intercollegiate athletics will go out of business," Weinberger countered.

I thought of the NCAA's fear one night in 2003 when I was covering a women's basketball game between the University of Connecticut and St. John's in Jamaica, Queens. The gym was filled with forty-five hundred people—including nine busloads of fans from Connecticut. The UConn women were ranked number one nationally, and were about to produce their sixtieth straight victory as part of their run to a second straight NCAA championship.

"My husband gave me these tickets for Christmas," one fan who had made the ninety-minute trip by bus told me. "You can't buy tickets for women's basketball in Connecticut. There just aren't any available."

The end of sports, indeed.

But it's instructive to go back to those first nervous moments to see how people reacted, and how many journalists responded. First of all, there was no national women's voice in sports then. So most of the quotes came from those who supported men's sports programs, virtually all of them against Title IX, which I'm sure they saw as invading their fiefdoms.

An NCAA lawyer claimed, "This may well signal the end of intercollegiate athletic programs as we have known them," and the rulings, he said, were like "throwing the baby out with the bath water."

What I discovered, however, was simply confusion, in Washington and at the colleges, that still makes Title IX controversial after all these years. It mandated that scholarships be offered to women on a percentage basis of the participants; that separate teams for women had to be created if a "significant segment" of female students wanted them. So a school like UCLA, which at the time Title IX was enacted spent 6 percent of its athletic budget on women's sports, had to come around dramatically. One school that got it from the beginning was St. John's. That day in 1973, I called the school's athletic director for comment on Title IX. His name was Jack Kaiser, and he told me the school already had changed the status of women's teams from "club" to "varsity." Then he added, "We now have women at our varsity dinner and other functions." It was a somewhat patronizing comment, to be sure. But remember the context of the times. Few realized then how many other functions there would be, and I certainly never envisioned that one day I'd be at St. John's in a packed gym, hearing fans yell for their women's team to "think tough," or "use your elbows," or "drive up the middle."

Still, the times were a-changin', as someone said. You just had to be perceptive enough to see it. I guess I'm smarter now than I was then.

I wound up writing often on issues affecting women in the sports world. One that remains significant concerns the issue of male athletes and rape.

Certainly the story I wrote about this had a palpable impact—Page One. By the 1990s, we were reading increasingly about athletes behaving badly. Was this merely because we were entering the electronic universe, and so stories and police reports flew around the country more quickly? Or was something else going on in sports?

My piece, appearing prominently in a prominent newspaper, gave credence to the shouts of many women's groups and rape-crisis counselors, whose pleas often had been ignored. I tried to detail not merely the numbers of reported attacks—a tricky bit of business, since most rapes are not reported—but also looked at the ways the entitlement of the male athlete often led to sexual abuse.

A digression: *Cosmopolitan* called and asked me to expand on the issue in a piece for which they would be paying a hefty sum. But Cosmo had a strange spin on it—they wanted me to describe some of the attacks, and what the women said about them. Essentially, they wanted me to write a titillating expose. I don't know why I was so surprised. The magazine, which professed a seriousness under editor Helen Gurley Brown, had always been about coy ways of catching your man. I learned that even so-called feminists could have a seamy side.

Still, the entire issue of athletes and sexual abuse really was part of a broader look at a national problem. And changes took place. Indeed, Richard Lapchick, the director of the Center for Sport in Society at Northeastern University when my *Times* piece appeared, told me that because of it, the United States Marine Corps began a program of sensitivity training to ease the transition into a gender-neutral force. Rookies coming into the National Football League attend a seminar in which the subject of proper reactions to, and relationships with, women are discussed by experts. Virtually every major university athletic program includes such a seminar as well.

But until the next headline, the subject generally is forgotten in the newspapers. Because of the constraints of daily journalism, stories often have a short shelf life. You write a piece, evoke wide-ranging comment, concerned organizations and individuals get a hearing, and then everyone goes on to the next subject. Indeed, that is almost the essence of what we do in the business.

There remains in the field of reporting women's sports a difficult tightrope act: except for writing about some superstars—say the Williams Sisters, or Jennifer Capriati, or the track hero of the moment—there has been a decided lack of in-depth personal discussion. I don't say there hasn't been any—but it certainly is much less than the male athlete. I believe much of this has to do with access, as well as—and this may be blasphemous—the possibility that coaches and athletic directors of women's sports may be concerned about being more decorous.

When I tell friends of a certain age that I, and my female colleagues, interview naked male athletes in the locker room, my pals are bemused and amused. Life—at least life up until the 1970s—decreed a certain decorum when it came to the usually mundane, but often important, locker-room interview we as sportswriters take for granted. But things have changed (as you might have noticed). We take seriously women athletes now; they are not merely a curious adjunct to men's games. And people such as the puissant tennis-playing Williams sisters are given the same psychological evaluation (my literature background, of course, prepares me for this ability) as their male counterparts.

Just look at developments in the twenty-first century:

* A woman coached a major college men's basketball team for the first time when Teresa Phillips took over for the suspended male coach at Tennessee State.
* A woman played in a men's PGA Tour event for the first time in fifty-three years when Annika Sorenstam teed off in the 2003 Colonial.
* Another woman golfer, Suzy Whalley, qualified for and played in the Greater Hartford Open that same year.

Yet, despite these recent dramatic crossovers, there is one area that remains largely out of bounds to me, as well as my male and female colleagues—the women's locker room. I cannot interview most women athletes in their lair—but women sportswriters routinely have access to male athletes in their locker rooms.

Thus, I find my job limited in a very important way when I write about college women athletes, or winter sports stars such as figure skaters. Two notable sports exceptions are the WNBA, which allows invasions by writers of both sexes before and after basketball games, and the WUSA, the soccer league. The United States Open (in Godless New York) is the only event on the tennis tour that allows men into women's locker rooms—although most male reporters skip the opportunity. We are not all a bunch of leering louts, after all. And on the women's golf tour, only its open championship allows men and women to enter even an adjacent area to the locker.

So what's the big deal about not being able to get into all women's locker rooms?

Well, in my own experience interviewing athletes, most of the actual dialogue took place in a locker-room setting. And it has been extremely important. Because of that access, the reader has benefited. Indeed, many of the behind-the-scenes revelations and much of the talk and chit-chat that is so important in journalism these days happens because reporters talk to athletes in the one place where there is more time to spend with them.

There was the moment Joe Namath threw a game-losing interception and then wailed in the locker room, "I stink." In locker rooms I have seen hockey goalies throw up; have seen a team president, quite drunk, deliver a between-periods lecture to his troops; have seen Walt Frazier chuckle and anoint future Senator Bill Bradley as "Dollar Bill" while Bradley basked in the afterglow of his Knicks' debut; have seen the late Yankees' manager Billy Martin stash his empty wine bottle in the trash basket under his desk.

I have never seen a moment like this in women's sports because for the most part I'm not permitted to.

Yet wouldn't it be fun to write—and read—about these kinds of moments that women athletes must endure, or go through, too? I would have loved to have been there when Tonya Harding and Nancy Kerrigan faced off in the 1994 Winter Olympics after Ms. Kerrigan was knee-capped by a Harding factotum.

By not being permitted in the locker room, we are limiting our perceptions of the entire event. Right now, we can write about what we see between the lines. Granted, for most of the twentieth century that was enough—it was what readers expected. But no more. For better or worse, readers expect behind-the-scenes gossip, insights gained away from the playing field—information they have not seen on Channels 2 through 96.

I decry the injustice—especially since I played a role in getting women into the building in the first place. Now, we wait outside. When jockey Julie Krone (the only female rider at Aqueduct then) came out of her private locker room, I interviewed her in the hallway. When I was at the game at St. John's where top-ranked Connecticut played, all of us interviewed players in a media room, away from the intimacy of a locker room. There, the coach sat nearby; the women gave us platitudes. This happens all the time when we are put in formal situations after women's events: we writers sit on chairs. The athletes are in the front of the room at a table. It's something like a classroom rather than an intimate give-and-take.

Do I really need to be in a woman's locker room? That isn't the question. It's a matter of equal access, isn't it?

To take another view of this, though, it could be argued that America's relationship with female athletes is in a nascent stage—just as was our relationship with male athletes into the 1960s. It will require a period of developing a fan base and building the athletes up as idols before readers care enough for the locker-room chatter.

Anyway, after all these years writing sports, I think it would be neat to be given the opportunity. But I wouldn't want to make a federal case out of it.

Then again, I wonder: perhaps there really is some fundamental difference in the way men and women behave, despite legislation that would close the gap. And some part of me believes that a majority of women believe that, too.

6

Present at the Creation

Sports has helped give me a worldview, almost as if I had studied international relations. I believe you can tell something about a country's character by the games it plays—or at least tell something about forces that shape the country.

Look at the European style of soccer—long passing, concentration on defense. Look at European history—broad swaths of action; a tradition of war. Then concentrate on the carioca style of Brazilian soccer, say—the intricate, close-weaved passing patterns, the head-fake. Smaller wars, tighter play. A sensuous culture that loves rhythm. At least, that's my interpretation—and I'm sticking to it.

Watching these "foreign" (at least to me, once) games, or writing about the new landscape of sports in America, and the world, has allowed me to venture into areas—often intruding where I wasn't wanted—that I had no knowledge of even as a sports fan. In fact, some of these areas didn't even exist, or certainly weren't part of our consciousness, when I was a youngster:

* International play involving American teams.
* I learned about unions and agents and expansion leagues.
* I was forced to find out about big-time college recruiting.

Remember the first time you saw a great foreign film? You asked yourself, "How long has this been going on?" Case in point: soccer.

As a young reporter in the 1960s, I jumped from sport to sport. I had played some intramural soccer in college and also had attended a few soccer games in the city's ethnic neighborhoods, which is essentially where the game was, and still is, played in New York—at little parks in the Bronx, in Astoria, Queens, on Randalls Island in the East River. I had covered Gaelic football games that attracted more fans. But then a promoter had an idea: bring to Yankee Stadium the most famous athlete in the world, Pele, the Brazilian soccer star, in an exhibition. The reasoning seemed to be sound. ABC had televised the World Cup soccer championships and had garnered impressive ratings.

In the States we had the brash, loudmouthed Cassius Clay, not yet a world figure; we had the young Jets quarterback Joe Namath, who sported white shoes; we had a host of aging superstars in baseball and basketball. Perhaps America was ready for another sport, the world's game. That was the fervent hope of the people who looked at soccer as the next big thing.

Pele's news conference at the fabled 21 Club attracted an international cast of reporters, one of whom began his questioning with "Honorable sir." Clearly, this fellow Pele was something more than merely famous to the rest of the world. He was addressed as "sir."

I understood, as a reporter, that the exhibition game was momentous around the world, for the United States was the last major world power that cared little for soccer. What happened in America was important all over the world—the Japanese and the French were wearing made-in-America jeans and T-shirts; our jazz musicians were playing in clubs from Amsterdam to Jakarta. The world was watching. I knew that I had to get this right when I wrote my story.

It may sound silly, but I went to the library and took out a book on soccer. I wanted to get some of the terms just right—corner kick, midfielder, "carding" (the referee holds up a card when a player is guilty of a serious violation). I wanted to use terms that were part of the sport's lexicon, but still not obscure the story for American sports fans. Also, I wanted to show I understood the nuances of the Brazilian game, so I called a journalist from a Brazilian news agency. I learned about "banana kicks" (shots that curve), and Pele's nicknames ("The Black Pearl" was one). My plan was to use occasionally an arcane word, but describe it in context so that it was self-explanatory. I approached this game like a social studies test.

In the midst of the hoopla of the exhibition game, of a media event that attracted United Nations officials and frenetic television crews from Brazil and the world's major soccer powers, it was a shoeshine man who made the event even more special for me.

It was at the Stadium that I renewed an old acquaintance—Rodney. I had not talked to him since the sixth grade, when I was twelve years old. He seemed a pleasant enough kid back then. He was black, I was white, and we didn't run in the same circle. Oh, I had seen him often in the shadow of the elevated train station—the "el"—five blocks from my house, shining shoes. But I felt embarrassed to talk to him in what I figured were his straitened circumstances. So it was almost twenty years before we hooked up again.

This time, he was at one of the Yankee Stadium gates, where he had become a fixture. He made a deal with a ticket-taker. Rodney found a thousand fans who were standing at the end of long lines. "Give me six bucks," he told each of them as he escorted them to his special entrance. They each went through as Rodney gave the ticket-taker three dollars for each fan smuggled in. Rodney made three thousand dollars that day.

The police subsequently told me that Rodney was the biggest sports ticket-scalper in New York City. He was proud of his apartment, which featured African masks and paintings. He enjoyed his furniture, his color television set. I asked him his story, and for old times' sake he related it to me:

His father was a cop, his mother a nurse's aide at Coney Island Hospital. His father was kicked off the force, though, after it was discovered he had "two families," in Rodney's words. Rodney learned he had fourteen brothers and sisters. He went to high school for six months, although I didn't recall seeing him there. "I had trouble reading," he said. "I wasn't stupid. I just couldn't read." So he went back to shining shoes full-time, until, he said, "some Jewish guy" told him about the money to be made scalping tickets. When you and I think about a ticket-scalper we might simply relate it to a Broadway show, or a World Series game. Rodney took it beyond that.

"I scalped the Pope," he said, very proudly. At the Pope's historic visit to the Stadium, Rodney went to dozens of churches in New York and asked if anyone there had a ticket for the event. He dressed neatly, if a bit raggedly. He had worn sneakers, but he said "please" and "thank you" and wound up with a few hundred tickets for the Pope's visit.

Eventually, Rodney employed "diggers," kids he recruited from Brooklyn and the Bronx to stand in line at special events and buy tickets, or he himself would knock on the door of school buses outside of the Stadium and ask whether there was an extra ticket.

"Schoolkids are always getting sick," he explained. "So their teachers always had an extra ticket or two." His great score was in the future: the night of the Ali-Frazier meeting at the Garden, he claimed to have made thirty thousand dollars.

As for Pele, Rodney had a good day's receipts from his partial take of the forty-five thousand fans. Some other people besides Rodney enjoyed that throng: American promoters were so entranced with the size of the crowd that they decided to form a professional soccer league. Before it even got off the ground, a rival league was formed. Thus, America, which never had organized soccer on a big-league basis, suddenly had two leagues. Don King was right: only in America.

It said something about American entrepreneurial spirit and its galloping optimism. It also foreshadowed rival leagues in other sports. What I realized immediately, though, was that the attendance at American soccer was almost directly proportionate to the ethnic makeup of the city: thus, an Italian team attracted more people than a British team in New York, a Latin American team more than one from Scotland.

I became the paper's soccer writer for a while. Perhaps I should have been more forgiving. The coach of one of the New York teams, a Briton named Freddie Goodwin, called me and asked why I was writing so negatively about his team.

"But, Freddie," I countered, "you know you've got a bunch of second-rate players." He agreed, but still couldn't understand an American reporter's objectivity. Still, soccer became popular in this country. Eventually the world's most attractive stars—including Pele—were given lucrative contracts to play in the States full-time. Soccer was expanding so rapidly, to more than twenty cities, with the flagship New York Cosmos leading the way, that the publisher E. P. Dutton asked me to do a book called *A Thinking Man's Guide to Pro Soccer*. It was scheduled to come out at the peak of soccer's popularity, and I dutifully quoted the league's marketing manager, who predicted it would be bigger than football. "After all," he said, "every boy in America can play soccer. Size doesn't matter." (Of course, this was many years before women's soccer became a major event.) What the marketing man didn't realize was that while everyone could play soccer, not many people talked about it once their playing days were through. And while soccer moms and dads would gladly go to see their own children play, it was quite something else for them to put down money to see unknown foreigners—albeit expert performers—play the game.

So my book came out in 1980—to my dismay, just in time to herald the death of big-time soccer in the United States. Since then the sport has returned on a more modest niche level, where I believe it belongs and where I hope it succeeds. Even if my book didn't. By the way, I hope Rodney has done well, too.

The last time I saw him, I was jogging around the Superdome in New Orleans the day before a Super Bowl. He was walking between two men.

"Rodney—how's it going?" I asked as I trotted over to him. One of the men put up his hands, like a stop sign. "Don't come any closer," he said. "This man is under arrest."

So Rodney was still working. I was glad for that.

At about the time of soccer's attempt to secure a foothold in the States, I was in Boston for a big week: Stanley Cup hockey and the Boston Marathon in 1967. I heard about a strange situation involving the Red Sox's Ken "Hawk" Harrelson, who had been traded to the Indians.

He didn't want to go to Cleveland. That was silly, I thought. Where else could he go? There was baseball's odious reserve clause, which bound a player to his team in perpetuity—but they could trade him whenever they wanted.

A fellow identifying himself as Harrelson's "agent," Bob Woolf, invited me up to his office. Until then, the only agents I was aware of in the sports business were guys who brought endorsements or speaking engagements to players. Woolf was different. He was involved in

Harrelson's baseball and personal life. Woolf told me Hawk would quit rather than go to Cleveland. That was absurd. The Indians wouldn't fall for that. I had never heard of a ballplayer who quit rather than accept a trade (Curt Flood's time was just around the corner). Woolf's ploy worked, however. Harrelson, who said he was ready to go into the restaurant business, went to Cleveland only after getting more money out of the deal than his original contract called for.

But that wasn't the story. This "agent" was. Woolf told me that my article on him in the Sunday *Times* had generated more than two hundred phone calls from players in all sports, asking him about representation. This was, unbelievably, a virtual first for most athletes. An agent? Why, the sports world knew that when one of Vince Lombardi's Packers had gone into his office and said he had an agent who would negotiate for him, Lombardi picked up the phone, said something to the person at the other end, and then handed the phone to the player. "Here," said Lombardi. "Talk to your new team. You've just been traded."

Woolf was to become the first major agent in the history of American sports. Yet when he began, owners wanted nothing to do with him. His first client was a Red Sox pitcher named Earl Wilson. The Red Sox refused to meet with Woolf. When Woolf also signed on the Celtics' John Havlicek and visited general manager–coach Red Auerbach to discuss salary, Auerbach practically jabbed Woolf with a cigar.

"He said he would not talk to me," Woolf told me. But Bob had an engaging personality—he never, ever made it personal when he negotiated with an adversary—and eventually people listened to him.

I don't know whether two hundred athletes did in fact call him following my piece—it would have been like Bob to say something like that to make me feel like a big shot. Eventually, he not only represented sports superstars such as Carl Yastrzemski and Larry Bird but also moved into show business with Larry King and even was the agent for a book written by the widow of President Anwar al-Sadat of Egypt.

Bob's success was so stunning that many law schools began offering courses in sports law. Every sports attorney (as he liked to call himself) since has acknowledged gratitude for his starting a remarkably lucrative adjunct to the games we play. In *Jerry Maguire,* the hero mentions his mentor, the first sports agent, named Dickie Foxx—who presumably is based on Woolf.

Bob let me view contracts of players he was negotiating for. I knew, of course, that he was hoping I would help make his case by writing about the low salaries those scurrilous owners were paying his near indigent clients. I got as expert reading a contract as a box score. In one golden moment, Bob even gave me the complete salary list of Major League Baseball—which included bizarre contract clauses such as the size of a hotel bed a player insisted he be given, and the amount of money toward dental school tuition one pitcher got for his wife. I loved all of it— even though it was sportswriting as I had never written it before. No one had ever taught me, nor any of us, about this. In fact, when I went on to teach journalism in college, I made sure to include something about contracts.

The tumultuous sixties helped give rise to the role of the agent because sports were expanding all over the map, new leagues were being formed, and players suddenly found themselves the objects of desire by rival leagues. Not only players were entering this brave new world. A new breed of owner was, too. Favorable tax laws made sports ownership a financially rewarding as well as heady experience. You could depreciate the value of a player while your franchise was increasing in value, often exponentially. And postwar economic expansion had created new millionaires wanting to do something for fun with their money.

One of these was a women's-clothing manufacturer named Roy Boe, who wound up owning the New York Nets, an American Basketball Association team on Long Island. The ABA was trying desperately to compete with the firmly established NBA. The Nets had a nationally recognized figure in Julius Erving—the nonpareil "Dr. J" (represented, coincidentally, by Woolf at one point in his career). But Boe had such tremendous money problems that, on the eve of the Nets moving to New Jersey and gaining a big-league image, he was forced to sell Erving to the Philadelphia 76ers. Thus, the Nets lost their franchise player, but Boe remained afloat for a while, eventually having to sell his Islanders' hockey team as well. Dr. J had become a legend by then, and in a few years the Islanders were to become one of the great teams in the history of hockey. Boe didn't share in any of it. His was one of the cautionary financial tales of the go-go era, when entrepreneurs simply assumed they could go into sports, become local celebrities, and have a franchise growing in value.

Some years later I thought it would be instructive to have lunch with Boe and write about his experience and what it had taught him. We went to the Yale Club. In the middle of the meal, a man came over and started to ask Boe some questions. I tried not to listen.

When the visitor left, Boe had a smile. "Who was he?" I asked.

"Oh, a dentist," said Boe. "He wanted my opinion on investing in a soccer team in Philadelphia."

Every few years, the major newspapers and magazines such as *Sports Illustrated* look into college recruiting. The stories create significant buzz, uncover surprising scandals, maybe even result in a new NCAA bylaw. Then, as in so much of journalism, the story fades.

Back in 1974, we were determined once and for all to do the definitive story on college recruiting with a multi-part series. College sports was booming, just as pro sports was expanding. Increasingly, the public was concerned about just who was recruited for colleges, while at many jock schools the alumni screamed for better teams. This was a difficult juggling act for America's universities—be inclusive, field better athletic teams, share the increasing wealth television was granting to the best sports schools.

We brainstormed about just what the series was going to be about. Someone came up with an idea that I didn't think could work: why not go out on a recruiting trip with a recruiter—visit the high school star, hear what the recruiter promises. I just never thought any college coach would go for that, whispering sweet nothings into the ear of a high school star while a reporter sat and listened to the pitch.

The most celebrated basketball player in New York then was a guard from DeWitt Clinton High School named Butch Lee. I called his coach and asked him about the colleges that were recruiting him. One of them was Marquette, in Milwaukee, and in fact the assistant coach was coming to New York in a few days.

Marquette was coached by Al McGuire, a wisecracking, sidewalks-of-New York guy. His brother Dick had played for the Knicks in the fifties. So had Al. I remembered him as the worst shooter on the team, but feisty. Another brother, Pep, owned a well-known bar in Rockaway, Queens.

Figuring I had no shot at listening in, since I assumed that a recruiter's pitch included some murky promises he wouldn't want me to hear, I still called Al. We had a great talk about recruiting. He told me his assistant, Rick Majerus, was coming to New York to interview Butch.

"Can I come along?" I asked. "Sure," he replied. He told me he'd get Majerus to call me and set up a meeting at the principal's office.

Majerus was a fellow who had given his life to basketball. He loved to analyze a player's rotation on the ball when he shot it. He could assess a player in seconds. When he called, I asked him what he did as an assistant.

"When you hear a college basketball team has an assistant head coach," he explained, "it means he's the recruiter. Nothing more. He goes out and gets the talent."

I went up to the high school one morning, when Lee was going to meet with Majerus, while the principal looked on. They allowed me to tag along. Lee was an amiable teenager and listened thoughtfully as Majerus made his pitch. Then Lee asked Majerus what Milwaukee was like.

"Butch," he said, "you're going to like Milwaukee. It's like a small New York."

Lee also wanted to know about McGuire's commitment to the program. Already, there were rumors that McGuire was looking elsewhere. "You'll play for Al McGuire," Majerus promised.

Then we went down to the gym. Lee picked up a basketball and took a few shots. Then he made a few passes. "He's the best high school guard I've seen this year," said Majerus after about two minutes.

After the workout, I went with Lee to his home in Harlem. We walked up a flight of stairs. I asked about the scholarship offers. He showed me his bedroom, which had a bare bulb hanging through a crack in the ceiling. He peered under the bed and pulled out some old Converse sneakers boxes. They were overflowing with letters from all over the United States. Many of the letters were handwritten from coaches of major basketball powers.

I decided to continue the interview at a restaurant. We went out for a steak dinner, and started to talk about how he was doing in school. He said he had an 84 average.

"What's your favorite class in school, Butch?" I asked.
"English is my most best subject," he replied.

It has remained one of my favorite quotes. I wonder how many kids for whom science was their most best subject got scholarship offers—but that's naive of me. Butch went on to star at Marquette, which won the NCAA championship (McGuire then immediately left). Butch also played basketball for the Puerto Rico Olympic team (a grandparent came from the island, which made him eligible). Majerus became the head coach at the University of Utah, still in love with the game. And DeWitt Clinton has produced more players who made it to the NBA than any other high school in America. I don't know how many grammarians the school has produced.

That same year, I thought about the contrast between journalists as do-gooders and their true role. This too had to do with a high school basketball star.

His name is still known to most basketball fans—Moses Malone. He had a C average in high school, but could he play b-ball! In fact, one-fourth of all the basketball-playing colleges in America wrote to him—three hundred letters in all. I guess they all were hungry for a C student, perhaps to upgrade their general GPA.

I was invited to a news conference in the city—the Utah Stars of the ABA were announcing they were signing him. His agent was on hand. No high school basketball player had ever jumped directly into the pros. Of course, almost thirty years later, in 2003, a high school player from Ohio named LeBron James was daily front-page news in sports because of his decision to go to the pros; he caused a flap when he accepted a jacket from a sporting-goods store, and there was another issue over how his mother could afford to buy him a Hummer, and whether she illegally accepted money from an agent to do so. But Moses in his day created an even bigger stir. There was the matter of honor: he had promised to attend the University of Maryland. Instead, he got an agent and accepted a pro contract with a potential worth of three million dollars. He even would get thirty thousand extra for every year he completed of college—an incentive, they said, to go to school.

One of the newspeople at the news conference was outraged. He was Jim Bouton, the former pitcher for the Yankees whose best-selling book *Ball Four* helped create a genre of tell-all sports autobiographies. He wrote about his carousing teammates such as Mickey Mantle and Whitey Ford. Bouton had become a sports anchor for the local CBS affiliate, Channel 2. And he repeatedly questioned the agent, the owner, Malone, and his mother about the fact that the youngster was giving up college in favor of pro ball. That night an outraged Bouton went on television to tell everyone about this awful event that was unfolding. Imagine: a kid with a C average not going to college. Some columnists were similarly outraged in their newspapers the next day. It was as if Malone would be going into a godless world in which his soul was damned, instead of the pristine, ivy-covered world of the colleges, where it would be saved.

Now, college might be a better choice than a nine-to-five job flipping burgers for a budding mathematician, say. But, really—what good would college do for Malone, other than perhaps enhance his pro value years down the road? And what if he got injured in school? His value as a pro would have plummeted.

Instead, it was very clear and simple to me: Here was a nineteen-year-old (a bit old for high school, but that's probably another story) with a supposed C average, whose mother earned one hundred dollars a week as a packer in a supermarket—and he was signing a multimillion-dollar deal. What's the question? If you were a financial adviser and told him to go to college instead, you'd be hauled in for malfeasance.

This was, to me, another instance of knee-jerk journalism, as if our responsibility as reporters was to ensure that everyone gets a college education, and that there is something inherently wrong with opting for money instead of school. How many law firms, or even newspapers or television stations, were offering college graduates a deal similar to Malone's?

While Malone eschewed college for a few million dollars, a nagging thought kept intruding in the back of my mind: I did not have a college degree, despite my standing in the newspaper community, despite the fact I had written four or five books at the time, despite the fact that I was teaching college journalism as an adjunct associate professor and my students called me "professor." Our three young children were still many years away from applying for college, but my wife had kept after me to return to college and get the degree.

"What will you put down under 'education' when they ask for the father's background on our children's college applications?" she was fond of saying. " 'College dropout?' "

I had started teaching at St. John's University, in its sports administration program. I had the idea for a course called "Current Issues in Sports"—it covered an array of the new issues that included women in sports, race, funding, agents. I expanded it eventually into a general course of journalism—how to write a story, a headline, where to get information, writing under deadline pressure. I used to take the students to games, or brought in athletes or club officials to talk to them.

I liked the kids at St. John's, but not the size of the classes—two dozen or more students. Marking papers was taking up too much time. The decision to leave was made easier for me when the school's noted basketball coach, Lou Carnesecca, asked me to do him a little favor. One of his starters was in my class. We were going into a school break and the student was a little behind in his work. However, the team also was about to play in a major tournament.

Louie called me. Could I excuse his player from writing a report over the break so that he could devote his time to the tourney? Funny—this was exactly the kind of thing that I had been writing stories about: schools cutting corners for their athletes, the sense of entitlement, the abandonment of standards when it came to some sports stars.

This was a dilemma. For simply on a human level, I liked Louie very much. Put aside the fact I was a reporter and in the past had interviewed him. He was a good man whose coaching instincts were to get the best for his players. No one confused Lou Carnesecca with, say, a professor of philosophy. On the other hand, hadn't I been the guy doing investigative pieces on high school and college corruption, and appearances of impropriety?

I thought about my situation. I realized that the basketball player in my class had been pushed up by one teacher after another, from grade school on, and now he was a senior in college, could barely do the work, and the problem now was in my lap. How many other similar student-athletes were there in America; how many professors were letting them slip through?

Well, I don't know if you could say I took the easy way out. Or maybe there was no easy way out—just the right way. But at the same time, it seemed to me that other teachers along the way had had a responsibility to the student, and had blown it. Was my stance going to change the system that had brought him—and me—to this point? I didn't think so. And there was another factor that had entrapped me. I had become part of the St. John's sports vortex. I didn't like to be sucked into it, and it left me with no alternative: I finished the term and left the school. I started a course in journalism at Adelphi University on Long Island, where the kids dressed a little neater, the classes were smaller, and there were no nationally ranked teams.

While I was teaching, I remembered my wife's admonition. So I went back to City College of New York and got my degree. It was twenty-one years after I had started college. Ironically, the graduation ceremonies were held at Madison Square Garden, where I had covered so many major sports events over the years. There I was, though, finally a participant on the floor of the most famous arena in the world. Up in the stands (my contacts at the Garden enabled me to get house seats) my wife, children, and in-laws watched me and waved.

Later, we went to dinner at the Midtown restaurant, Mamma Leone's, where I also had attended many press conferences and sports luncheons. My wife had told them I was celebrating my graduation. When the waiter brought the cake that read "Happy Graduation" to the table, he set it down in front of eight-year-old Mark and started singing "Happy Graduation to You." After all, why would the waiter think a forty-year-old was graduating?

In any event, I now had the degree, but I learned about banana kicks and the sanctity of contracts out of school.

7

The Electronic Village

When I'm in front of the television watching the World Cup, or a heavyweight championship fight, or a Stanley Cup final, I still get electronic flashbacks—and for a moment, I envy the reporters who sit there with their laptops, press "send," and know that somehow, using a technology that is barely a generation old, their stories come to rest in a newsroom computer in about a second or two. These lucky stiffs today have an electric outlet at their desk—be it in a stadium in Seoul or a press box aerie in Detroit—a telephone connected to a simple plug-in outlet, a computer that will dial "9" to get an outside line.

I guess I was an earthbound pioneer. Back in 1974, the *Times* was fiddling around with something it called "automation." I was known as the guy who could always get the story. On a bus trip with the Rangers Fan Club to Montreal, I cajoled the driver to pull over on the New York State Thruway so I could file my story at a telephone booth; I was dogged, once calling the home of the Yankees' new manager twenty times in one night so I could get confirmation on his status. I had found phones in unlikely places for stories on billiards. I had worked under the pressure of writing at ringside at Madison Square Garden, where I pounded away on my metal Olivetti, handed the copy to a Western Union telegrapher, who used Morse Code to transmit the story back to my office in Times Square. There, another telegrapher translated the code into a typewritten story. So the paper, knowing I wasn't afraid of a challenge, asked me to use this "computer" and write a story about a fledgling outfit called the New York Stars of the World Football League. They were practicing out in Oakdale, far out on Long Island.

I was also accustomed to using the phones if there were no telegrapher handy. Thus, if the computer did not work, I could simply call in my story. Back then, we had a phone room, staffed by three or four people who tape-recorded your story as you spoke it, then transcribed it. This time I was equipped with a twenty-pound box I dubbed the "blue monster." Micro-chips? It had a four-inch screen and somewhere in its innards was a little tape cassette—you know, like the ones that played Perry Como songs.

I had to rent a motel room, where I sat and wrote my story after attending the team's football practice. The football office didn't have room for my computer. The click of the keys was more muted than my clattering Olivetti, and the words on the screen seemed strangely out of place, as if they were floating in air. But soon I was finished.

Now, for the transmission.

The story was being sent back to the newsroom on West 43rd Street, where our legendary editor, A. M. Rosenthal, was monitoring it. He stood at a computer along with an affable fellow named Chick Butsikares, who had an interest in things electronic, so I guess they figured he'd be the perfect inside guy to see how this was working out. Also, someone from the computer company was there.

This was the trio that was about to receive the first computer-generated story at the venerable paper. It was not without some sense of history that I set to work. I had known that the *Times* had a scoop on the sinking of the *Titanic* back in 1912 because it alone among the other newspapers had monitored the newfangled wireless transmissions from the ship. When the ship's transmissions stopped, the *Times* realized that something had happened. Now, more than sixty years later, it had outfitted me with a contraption that had an external modem—that is, you took your phone off the cradle, dialed the New York City number, listened for the beep, and quickly pushed the phone into the cups on the computer. So I dialed, and heard some beeping sounds. I made the connection—and voilà—or Eureka! as someone might have put it one hundred years before—I got a "successful transmission" red flash.

***New York Times* editor A. M.
Rosenthal.** Photo courtesy of the
New York Times.

But not so fast. I called the folks at the other end for verification. They
told me, "Nothing received." I did it again. And again. When I called for
the third or fourth time, I heard Rosenthal chuckling. I had the feeling
Abe wasn't quite so sanguine about this automation business. Finally, I
asked someone: "Would that jackhammer pounding in the parking lot,
outside my motel window, impede transmission?" Indeed it could. It vi-
brated. Somehow, it jangled the nerves of the phone lines, as well as
mine. So I took off my shirt, baring my chest, put the phone back into
the cups, covered the phone with the shirt, and tried again. This time,
there were what I took to be sobs of delight on the other end. However
it worked, it worked, and my story still is available on microfilm.

My newspaper had entered the electronic age.

And yet—we didn't even have computers at the paper then. My
transmission had been translated into a code that went onto something
looking like a ticker tape, which was then fed into some reconfigured
linotype machine built in the 1920s. Indeed, it was to be another eight
years before we started to use computers in the field. In those first, halt-
ing moments I had my share of glitches. When you transmitted with an

external modem at a ball game, you had to make sure no one was going to hit a home run—or else the press box would be rocked by noise and vibrations of the fans' happy feet. And when I was in the Alps for the Winter Olympics, I had to make sure my phone cord was compatible with the French modules. Now, in places from Africa to Argentina, computer phone cords simply plug into the wall outlet, or into the phones themselves.

There was a moment we in the sporting fraternity still talk about: Shea Stadium in those early computer days had no phone lines in the second row of the press box. So reporters who weren't sitting in the first row asked a colleague to extend the phone line over the heads of people so it could be attached to the computers.

This was how the acerbic columnist, Dick Young, was filing his story. An unsuspecting writer walked down the first row, though, and his head inadvertently pushed the phone cord, disconnecting it. Young followed with a nonstop grab-bag of creative cursing that stunned even sportswriters. He wasn't the only one who had fumed at this brave new world. One reporter—from Philadelphia, I think—famously picked up his computer and threw it to the floor in anger. Others routinely gave theirs a whack to make it behave (actually, a sideways slap worked best on the Blue Monster).

As for me, I took some convincing. I had typed eight books and probably four thousand stories by the time they gave me a computer. I had always believed the tactile sense of paper helped the writing process. I wrote many obituaries, and felt that the serendipitous leafing through old stories yielded surprising nuggets of information. Quickly, though, I realized how we all were better served with this amazing device—how quickly I could file a story and get it to my office instantly, with no middle-men.

My most frustrating precomputer moment came when I was doing a light-hearted hockey column, and had called Charles Schulz, the creator of "Peanuts." Schulz was a great hockey fan, loved to play the game, and even had his own ice rink. I asked him what Snoopy was going to give the great hockey player, Gordie Howe, for Christmas.

"An elbow," was Schulz's whimsical reply.

Delighted, I wrote the piece, and dictated my story over the telephone to the paper. When you spoke your stories, you made sure you spelled out proper names, and in particular were careful of "m" and "n." For the vast majority of words, though, you took for granted that the operator had heard you properly and would faithfully record them. The next day I picked up the paper and turned to my column. I was shocked. For I read that Snoopy was giving Gordie Howe an "oboe."

Three days later, I got a letter from Schulz.

"That was the worst typo I have ever seen," he said. No wonder I love my laptop. But I've kept his letter.

In 1963, when I got my first boxing assignment in the old Madison Square Garden over on Eighth Avenue and 50th Street, I had a Western Union telegrapher sending my story in Morse code. At the other end, in the paper's sports department, another geezer from the railroad days of the 1920s transcribed the story, listening to it in Morse, and typing at the same time.

These old Western Union telegraphers used to come to work with their black "keys" in an old cigar box. They'd plug in the key at ringside, where I'd write my story. Seven blocks farther south, at the paper, another fellow took *his* key out of his cigar box, plugged in, and recorded the dots and dashes by retyping them in English. He then handed his copy, of my story, to a copy editor who checked it for accuracy, grammar, and space. The editor put a headline across the top and sent the piece by pneumatic tube to the composing room a floor above. There a linotype operator, on a machine that could have been forty or fifty years old, turned a series of levers, melted a "pig" of lead, and typed four or five words a minute, which came out in lead letters.

Every story, every day and night, for most of the twentieth century, came out this way at the *Times*—indeed, at most newspapers around the world. Now, I'm writing this on a computer that has so much memory it wouldn't even blink if each of the eight thousand–plus stories I've written were stored here.

But despite the genesis of the computer age, I often had to do things the old-fashioned way.

Lake Placid 1980: I was covering the United States hockey team's now-legendary route to capturing Olympic gold. I was seated in a balcony high above the ice. My only concern was how to get the damned story into the newspaper. We had one other reporter who knew how to use a new computer, which earned him passage to Lake Placid. The computer was a second-generation big blue thing. But there was no room for it in my dimly lit, musty aerie high above the ice. So I typed my story on my old Olivetti. Deadline time approached. Deadlines always loom, but in Lake Placid it was overbearing. Games would end about 10 P.M. My deadline was an hour later. I rushed down the stairs, past the crowds filing out, into an auditorium that served as a conference room, and waited for players and Coach Herb Brooks to make an appearance.

I left the news conference about 10:30. I ran up the stairs, out of breath, sat down, and in thirty minutes tried to capture the event, the importance, the crowd, the player reaction. Luckily, I had grown up in the business with shouts of "copy!" always in my ears. As a young reporter, I was given night rewrite. Often, I wrote twenty or twenty-five stories on a Saturday night. Not big ones, necessarily—but 69th Regiment Armory polo, or about someone named Kahn winning a squash racquets tourney, or the results of an Army-Navy dual track meet, or a cross-country run in Central Park.

I wrote fast even when I didn't have to write fast. And it became a game with me. No matter what, I knew I could get in the story—even one that ended at 10 P.M., sixty minutes before deadline. I was, I liked to believe, the fastest gun at the *New York Times*.

In fact, the closest I ever came to blowing a deadline was a 1981 Orange Bowl game starring an Oklahoma quarterback named J. C. Watts. He led a comeback, really, a sort of 1930s B-movie rah-rah college comeback, which screwed up my lead. I had to re-do it at the moment of deadline—but the paper made it. A year later, Watts was drafted by the Jets. At training camp I told the kid how he had almost made me mess up. He chuckled, and apologized. The rookie failed his tryout with the Jets—but went on to become a Republican congressman.

But this Olympic night, it was nearing 11 P.M., the latest I could file my piece. I crumpled up the story into a ball and threw it down below to Dave Anderson, our Pulitzer Prize columnist. Dave was standing in the mezzanine. He caught it on the fly, then took it down additional steps to the reporter at the computer, where it was retyped—and sent on its way over those newfangled phone lines. Thus the world learned about the Americans' victory over the Soviets in the *Times*.

No, I didn't have a sense that this miracle on ice was being born. All I remember was being in the balcony of a badly lit arena, working in cramped spaces. In fact, until I got back to my rustic, bare-bones motel room—I still remember the stuffed deer's head over the bathroom entrance—and watched the late news, I didn't even realize that this was a big deal to the rest of America.

After one of the United States' victories, I collared Brooks. He was a disciple of Machiavelli, and despised by many of his players. But we had developed a rapport because I was one of the few reporters who believed him when he said his team had a chance to defeat the Russians, maybe even go all the way. He had announced at a press conference after one of the victories that he had told his team, in a pregame pep talk, "You were born to be here."

"Come on, Herb," I whispered when I moved him away from the crush of writers. "You didn't really say that, did you?"

He reached into his shirt pocket and took out a folded piece of paper. He unveiled it to me. On it was written: "You were born to be here." Herb had let me in on a part of history—a quintessential moment of Americana.

In retrospect, I realize that television—and not the newspapers— made that team the icon it has become. At that point, not many people were interested in hockey in the States. In fact, ABC, which was televising the Soviet-U.S. game, didn't even put it on live. It was on tape. But the victory came at the time when America felt it was being held hostage by Iran, which had taken dozens of Americans from the U.S. embassy in Tehran, and there was a feeling of helplessness in this country. So when word spread through radio, and the TV news, that the United States had advanced to the gold medal game by defeating the Russians, an extraordinary number of people turned on their televisions to see the tape of the victory.

And in the final seconds, when the television announcer, Al Michaels, shouted, "Do you believe in miracles?" a legendary story was born. I wish I had realized that when I wrote my piece. Maybe I still was too old-world, too Timesian, and I was almost afraid to go overboard in writing this piece about a bunch of collegians defeating the best amateur team in the world. I really wanted to describe this as a sort of morality play, even beyond good and evil. I wanted to take this victory and put it in terms of lifting up America, which had been going through, in President Jimmy Carter's phrase, "a malaise." Instead, concerned about a fellow on our copy desk who was the point man in reading every important story, and who made every story come out the same, I turned in a pedestrian, if old-*Times,* lead about the "comeback" United States team. This was more than a comeback. It was a statement. I learned a lesson that day: write what you feel, and let the copy desk take out the adjectives if they must.

8

The Craft (Or Is it Art?) of Writing

We were taught at the *Times* to be extremely careful with words—as if we were in a lab handling a deadly virus.

If you were writing a hockey story, at all costs avoid the word "puck," which is like telling a football writer not to use the word "football." Puck, however, could be infamously misspelled by a linotype operator with a puckish sense of humor. As I recall, whenever there was a new union contract coming up, and the linotypers could be especially mischievous, we were reminded again about not putting the puck word in the paper.

In many ways, we were a prissy lot. We had a "slot man"—the chief copy editor—who changed a "revealed" on me. I had written about a club owner "revealing" how much the team's salary was.

"I prefer 'disclosed,'" the editor said. "'Reveal' to me means something like, a woman revealing her thighs."

So at the *Times,* we had a lot of sexual problems—not to say intestinal ones as well. And yet, at bottom was a mission to inform, but in a way that did not offend. Also, the fact that Timespeople all over the world adhered to the same tenets assured a uniformity of credibility, of accuracy, of sensibility. It extended far beyond words to avoid. There is a universe of "style" that governs how we write numbers, or terms of address, or names of gangsters. For example, in newspaper stories in France or in Moscow, in Brooklyn or in San Diego, you can pick "nine" apples—but not, say, "ten." Once you reach double digits, you use the numeral "10." The first time you refer to a person in the news pages, use the full name—Donna Shalala. But the next time, it's "Ms. Shalala." Sports was always an exception—it never was Mr. Mantle, or Mr. Tyson—except if the name appeared on the news pages, or, in Mantle's case, his obituary.

Sometimes, this creates unusual lexicography. You read about the notorious John Gotti being indicted, and in any subsequent reference it's "Mr. Gotti." When terrorists are arrested, they immediately become "mister" in the *New York Times.* My favorite *Times* moment in honorifics came the day after several Yankees, including Billy Martin, were arrested for a brawl at the Copacabana night club in Midtown Manhattan. On Page One, it was "Mr. Martin" after the first reference—until the story "jumped" to the sports pages. And then it was, simply, "Martin."

Today's sportswriters needn't worry about the strait-jacketing instructions I received before covering my first Madison Square Garden fight. Get this: I had to make sure that in my lead paragraph, I not only got in the name of the winner and his opponent but also how many rounds the bout had been scheduled for, what the attendance was, and whether the fight was on television or not—not to mention, the bout took place "last night." This answered the eternal verities of newspaperdom: who, what, why, when, where (and how). Of course, we went beyond that in producing the *Times.*

In baseball, for example, we had to mention which league the Yankees played in and their manager's name. These facts were, of course, known to every person who cared to read the story. But what it did, too, was allow the copy editor to fashion a headline with information that also was in the story. In other words, a headline never said anything that wasn't mentioned in the piece below. If I wrote, for instance, "The Yankees defeated the White Sox, 5–2, last night at the Stadium," that's an easy enough head to write. A Yankee story usually would be the lead story on a page, streaming across the top. But underneath that, there would be a smaller headline leading into the story itself. Now, you didn't want to use the word "Yankees" again. So if you were a copy editor, you might write "Stengel's men win in 9th." If I had never mentioned Manager Casey Stengel in my story, you couldn't use his name in the headline. All these constraints not only helped the copy editors create

Me and Casey Stengel, 1965.

headlines but also geared our stories to the symbolic readers we were always reminded about: the university professor and the little old lady in Keokuk, Iowa. This help for the headline writer also required us to describe a pitcher as either a right-hander or left-hander, and to note the number of paying fans (not "paid," I was admonished, because some readers might mistake that as meaning the fans had been paid to come to the game).

If I were writing about a horse race, I had to make sure the owner's and the trainer's names were included—as well as the exact payoff for a two-dollar bet, and the margin of victory. If I were writing about harness racing, in which horses either "trot" or "pace," I couldn't say a horse was a front-runner, since technically this was a gaited racer; it didn't "run," but paced or trotted.

I was, however, responsible for a change in one long-standing *Times* no-no: the way the word "veteran" was used. I had been told we never used the word to describe someone who was, well, a veteran player. Why?

Because readers could confuse that with thinking the athlete had been a veteran of World War II. That's right—there were no "veteran" ballplayers, no "veteran" goalies, even into the 1970s at my paper. Never mind that World War II had been over for thirty years, and no one was likely to think that we were referring to his military service when we described the "veteran" Hank Aaron. Yet when I took over the coverage of the Jets' football team in 1975, I found that the word "veteran" had been excised from my copy when I wrote about Namath. By this time in the history of American sports, the unions had become part of the equation. The word "veteran" had a specific meaning in major-league sports contracts and "veterans" had certain rights in becoming free agents, or receiving minimum guarantees of income.

I pointed this out to our sports editor. He brought it up with the guardians of *Times* style. I was stunned when I was upheld, and from that day on, you could be a veteran football player in the *New York Times.*

We may have been old-fashioned and slow to change, but we also were eclectic. Unlike the *Post* or *News,* we perceived our audience as including more than the basketball or hockey fan—the reader was a yachtsman or polo player or squash racquets aficionado, too. I had to learn all the arcane terms of these often arcane sports. Some I wrote about in person, such as the rugby match they always played during intermission of the indoor polo matches at the 69th Regiment Armory. Mostly, though, I was bombarded with stories on a Saturday night, since I was the junior reporter and had to serve my time in the office. You'd be surprised what went on during a Saturday in metropolitan New York.

We covered everything back then. If you sailed a boat and hauled out the spinnaker, if you slid the "rock" in curling, if you could spin the ball off the dedan in court tennis—and you were in a tournament—all you had to do was call me. I wrote about the longtime president of the National Hockey League, Clarence Campbell, who served as "skip," or captain, on his curling team and often played in New York; or about the court tennis setup at an exclusive Manhattan club—it emulated the type of tennis they used to play "at court" in medieval times, with its simulated palace grounds. "Frostbite racing" on Long Island Sound? Cross-country running in Central Park? Squash racquets, squash tennis, indoor handball, outdoor handball. Private golf club tournaments, fencing (was it foil, saber, or épée? I would ask), table tennis, billiards, darts, bowling, paddle tennis.

Soon, I knew all the terms, all the personalities who inhabited these universes of the Upper East Side, or exclusive suburbia, or some Brooklyn neighborhood—people such as George Skakel, the polo player (one of Ethel Kennedy's brothers; he died choking on a piece of steak); Ruby Obert, the legendary handball player; Bus Mosbacher, the yachtsman; and Pete Bostwick, the squash/golfer and amateur sportsman par excellence (he even won the French Amateur golf tournament).

(I know—you're asking about dog shows, motorcycle racing, indoor lacrosse, Demolition Derby. I've done them, too. I simply forgot.)

Hundreds, if not thousands, of people are hanging around the paper waiting to die. They may not even feel ill.

We have their stories—advance obituaries—in the computers. For many years a chap named Alden Whitman wrote the paper's major obituaries. We dubbed him "Mr. Bad News." But when world leaders heard him calling, they invariably gave him the time he needed to write their advance obits. They wanted to get their legacy right.

Most major papers will also do advances on young, healthy notables who suddenly become seriously ill, just in case they get worse. I have written at least a dozen not-yet-used "advance obits" on sports celebrities, mostly aging boxing figures. Over the years, I probably have written two dozen obituaries once someone has died.

You try to write an obituary the way you would write a profile—capturing the humanity of the person as well as the salient facts, and what made this person worth reading about. At my paper we have a couple of informational "must's" in obituaries—the person's date of birth, and full name. These aren't always available—sometimes the family doesn't even know or perhaps there are no immediate survivors who do. So we have to use resources. And twice, I have to admit, I actually had to ask someone for information I was using in his advance obituary, although he did not know it.

I was writing the advance for the octogenarian boxing matchmaker for Madison Square Garden, Harry Markson. I did not know his date of birth. That night, as it happened, I was at a dinner with him and he was sitting at my table. I used some excuse to get it. He rattled it off. I inserted it in my story. Another similar incident happened when I was writing about the famed boxing announcer Don Dunphy. We saw each other at a party, and I made some comment about us having similar birthdays. Actually, we didn't, but he told me his, and I had my little bit of information that the story required, without having to tell him it was for his death notice.

One advance obit I wrote cropped up in the strangest place—on safari in Africa. Leon Hess was an unusual man hardly known to the public. He ran the Amerada Hess company and you saw his name over every Hess gas station in the country. But he didn't like publicity, even though he also owned the New York Jets. He had dealt personally with Mu'ammar Gadafi in Libya over oil; he had been extremely close to the deposed Shah of Iran; he was a respected member of pro football's inner councils; he was a major behind-the-scenes political figure in New York City because of his campaign contributions. Before I left for the trip, I got word that Hess was ill and was being treated for some time. I updated his obituary before taking off for Africa.

One morning at our lodge, just having returned from safari, I picked up the daily newsletter that had been placed on the bed. Among the business stories was the obituary on Leon I had written.

But sitting in an office and trying to write something literary and journalistic about a celebrity is quite different from digging into a story about a young college student who died. At that moment in 1976, I hated what I had to do. The situation was this: a rower for Columbia University had been caught in a vortex of currents on the Hudson at the northern tip of Manhattan. It was in a place with a Dutch name that translates as the Devil's Spout. The boat was swamped, and abandoned by all nine oarsmen. Eight of them were able to make it to shore only sixty yards away.

I remember calling one of the crew, a teenager, really, and hearing the guilt in his voice as he spoke of having no idea his teammate was missing. But mostly, I remember asking the dead youngster's mother about her son—my conviction was that this was what I was supposed to do as journalist. Yet, what did I expect? A soliloquy? My call only furthered her unhappiness. How less anguishing it was to write obituaries about those who had lived full lives—Red Grange, Archie Moore, Dunphy and Markson.

And then there was a story that had tragic overtones, but turned out to be an uplifting event. By 1992, I had stopped covering the Jets. The 1989 season was my last. I used to tell people I was taking time off for good behavior, following fifteen seasons with one of the country's most schizophrenic teams.

It was late in the season, and I was writing a sidebar on a Jets-Chiefs game, glad I had decided not to cover the team on a regular basis. The third quarter was only a few seconds old when it happened—Dennis Byrd, the left end, was rushing Chiefs' quarterback Dave Krieg. So was Scott Mersereau, Byrd's teammate. But Krieg ducked under Mersereau's grasp, falling out of the way. The two linemen collided. The 266-pound Byrd drove his helmet into Mersereau's chest. Byrd lay motionless on the turf for several minutes as medical personnel quickly realized his lack of any movement signaled a serious problem.

"My neck is broken," Byrd finally said.

He was strapped onto a gurney and taken to the hospital. When the game was over, someone at my office asked me to do a story on Mersereau. I had known him since he joined the Jets during a strike of the regulars, a marginal player who had hung on. We had a good relationship, but at this moment in his life, while Byrd's future hung in the balance, I did not want to interview him. Yet, everyone was clamoring to speak to him, and Mersereau dressed by himself in a room away from the locker. Finally, I suggested to the other writers that perhaps I could get to speak to Mersereau alone, and I'd act as the pool reporter.

He had tears in his eyes as I sat down next to him. It was just starting to sink in: Byrd was his good buddy, a deeply religious man who was in a hospital room where they were drilling a "halo" into his skull; he might never walk again, might not ever have the use of his limbs. This was a time I felt like a vulture, felt I was invading another human's privacy. And yet, while I saw the human face, I also saw Mersereau as someone who had a story to tell, and this was what I do.

Coincidentally, my son Mark was at New York University Medical School then, but had been doing an internship in sports medicine at Lenox Hill Hospital—where Byrd was taken. I was not even aware that

Dennis Byrd, right, collides head-first with teammate Scott Mersereau, in a game in 1992 between the Jets and the Kansas City Chiefs. Courtesy of ABC Sports.

Mark was part of a team of doctors that had gone to see Byrd. I never asked Mark about any dealings he might have had with the Jets, and he never mentioned them to me. I had suspected this type of potential conflict could arise—Lenox Hill was the home base of the Jets' physicians, and I knew that once Mark had a working relationship with them, there could be times when it would be awkward. So I never asked him about anything to do with Lenox Hill. Some of the other reporters, though, staked out the hospital, hoping for word from the players who started to stream in the next day. Among the writers was Paul Needell of the *News*. He was an aggressive newshound. Indeed, he managed to work his way onto the same floor as Byrd's room.

Paul had a brainstorm to get inside the room, in a manner of speaking. He asked Byrd's teammate, Marvin Washington, to take in a tape recorder and interview Byrd for him. When Washington returned from the room he explained to Needell there were too many people inside, and he couldn't do the interview. Still, Needell felt confident he was getting inside stuff none of the other writers had. And then Needell saw my son Mark, wearing his hospital togs, coming out of Byrd's room with several other doctors. Needell's spirits sagged. With his tabloid sensibilities, he was convinced that Mark would share with me all the heart-rending information from inside that room.

That never happened. More important, Byrd made a wonderful recovery, able to walk, albeit with a limp. He got to hold his wife and child again, as he had prayed for on his way to the hospital.

Neither Needell nor I ever got the whole inside story. I'm glad I didn't.

There are some stories you get—or achieve greater insight into—because you've ingratiated yourself with the principals. Cover a heavyweight title fight, say, and most of the reporters are on equal footing. But then there are times when knowing just a bit extra is invaluable. That is why I always tell my students, and young reporters who ask, to get personal. You may not need to socialize with them, but get to know the athletes, or anyone else you write about, on a human level.

The 1980 Olympics was among the great experiences anyone in the newspaper business—especially sports—would have wanted. I was dealing with a group of spirited young athletes who quickly saw themselves on a mission. It was fun being around the hockey players and their scheming coach, Herb Brooks. Privately, he would call the Russians "bastards." Ask a question, and you got an unguarded response. Also, I had a fondness for hockey. It was my first beat, and I had always found the players an uncomplicated lot. Of course, in the days I covered them, they were all Canadians. When Americans and Russians and Finns and Czechs and Swedes made up almost 50 percent of the National Hockey League within twenty years, the simpler, old-world verities of the sport were replaced by a certain jazzed-up quality. Instead of some players being able to make it to the big leagues because they were "enforcers," everyone had to skate and shoot and do pirouettes. It changed from a cold sport to a hot sport.

Almost immediately, I went from writing about the highest form of amateur sport to writing about America's symbol of a professional team in the world of sports: the New York Yankees.

The worst assignments I have had in my career were those covering the Yankees, on the road, in the 1980s. I say worst because the Yankees were a daily Bronx Zoo story. They were New York's landmark team, which made them, it can be argued, the most important team in American sports. And of course by the 1980s, you had to hang out at the lockers, had to whisper to players what the manager said, had to get something the television viewers did not know, had to try to scoop the other reporters with whom you had just had dinner, had discussed your families and children. In other words, you had to try to screw your buddy.

This was a typical situation: Billy Martin, who had been the A's manager, was returning to Oakland, but this time as Yankees' manager. A group of fans—mindful of the fact that Martin had punched a marshmallow salesman in a bar—tossed marshmallows in his direction as he walked toward the dugout.

"What's happening to America?" Martin asked me as he spoke from the safety of his grungy office during a pregame tirade. "People have no respect for anything any more." I noticed that underneath Martin's desk, in a makeshift wine cooler—a trash can—two bottles of wine were sitting. During the game Martin often left the dugout and headed somewhere under the stands. When the game was over and I interviewed Martin in his office, I saw the bottles were empty and turned upside down.

I had gotten into a somewhat civil relationship with Martin. When the road trip was ending I told him I had enjoyed covering him. I had, too. He was charming when he wasn't being cynical, or threatening. When I got back to New York, I said, I was going on a trip to Spain.

"Say, would you bring me back one of those things they drink wine from?" he asked. "You know, they hold it like this." He was talking about a *bota,* the goatskin flask shepherds carried. Then he added, "If I'm not here, the Yankees will know where to send it."

Funny he said that. Martin was famous for getting fired every so often by the Yankees' uber-boss, George Steinbrenner.

I've thought often since then about what I would have written had this happened, say, last week rather than in the 1980s. I might have used his statement—"If I'm not here . . ."—because of the pressure I felt from my colleagues. For covering a major-league sports team is now writing about the wart on the face. Or the pimple on the ass. Of course, being around Martin, it was all about warts and pimples.

On a team flight somewhere in the Midwest, I heard a commotion. Goose Gossage had taken his food tray and thrown it up to the ceiling, splattering it with food after being annoyed that he had come in to the game late and given up a home run. Martin, sitting an aisle across from me, had been drinking since the flight took off. He got up, smiling, when he heard the commotion and staggered to the rear. Then he came back and said, in a long slurring of words, "Oh, he's just pissed off." Martin laughed.

Then there was the time Martin brought a girlfriend along on the trip, and she was sitting in a front-row seat just to the left of the Yankees' dugout. During the game, he often went out to talk to her, something I had never seen anyone, married or single, do before.

On one road trip, my office called me early in the morning. "Did you see the *Daily News*?" they asked me. It was rhetorical, since you usually don't get the *News* in a Minneapolis hotel. "It says George is about to fire Billy."

Not only that, there was a front-page cartoon by the clever Bill Gallo showing Martin about to be axed again. I knew that Steinbrenner enjoyed sending up trial balloons about Billy all the time. When the Boss was unhappy with his bad boy, he would say things to certain favored members of the press, who would use a blind item about Martin's imminent departure. Sometimes, it even happened.

I hated doing this sort of stuff. I knew Steinbrenner wouldn't level with me, but I called his office anyway. He didn't return the call. Then, somehow, I reached someone who worked in the club's front office. He loved the *New York Times*, luckily for me. He also happened to be the team's in-house legal counsel.

I asked him about the *News* story. "If it's going to happen, it hasn't happened yet," he said. "And I don't think it will. Any time you fire a manager, you've got to get all the legal stuff in shape. There's a contract to be paid off, and other things. It won't happen unless I know about it. I'll tell you what—if I hear anything, I'll call you."

I never heard from him, and Martin wasn't fired—at least not that time. So the next time I saw Martin, I gave him a Spanish *bota*. Except

Collector Barry Halper in his basement with Billy Martin. Courtesy of Barry Halper.

the next time I saw him wasn't the next year—he was fired. Not when the *News* said he'd be, but sometime the next season. I kept Martin's flask around, figuring he'd return. He did, a year or so later. I walked into his office with the *bota*.

"What's this?" he asked me. He had forgotten all about it. He took it and placed it in a drawer somewhere in his desk. That was the last time I saw Martin, who died a few years later—after he crashed his car near his house.

The comic and social commentator George Carlin has a delicious take on the difference between baseball and football. He describes baseball as pastoral, played in a "park," on "grass." Football, though, is something like warfare, played in a "stadium," on "turf." Despite my Martin moments, I agree with Carlin—I probably would have agreed with him even more forty or fifty years ago, when all baseball was played in the daytime. It has turned into a grind, but it has a certain rhythm in its intensity.

Because manager and players are occupied with an actual game 162 times a year, almost in an unbroken string, they try to maximize the noncompetitive parts of the day. Thus, as a reporter, I can saunter into a locker room at four o'clock in the afternoon and find players relaxing. In football, a reporter never talks to players before a game. The football locker room is closed to the news media until fifteen or twenty minutes after a game. Even that number is mandated by league rule so that the players can unwind.

Not only can you schmooze with the baseball players in the locker room, but in the pregame moments you can sit with them on the dugout bench, chatting them up before they go into the batting cage. You can walk between the dugouts at will, past players having a catch, or a coach hitting fungos to his outfielders. All this is necessary to a baseball writer, especially one for a morning paper. Remember, there is that early edition, which closes before the game has even started, and you must have an early story. Then there is the running story, and finally what we call the "final sub." The way baseball is today, the way radio and television and the newspapers are today, one observer's take—yours—on a game is hardly enough. You need many voices in a story, including the ballplayer and manager and sometimes coaches, too. In many cities, the talk-radio heads are more famous than the newspaper reporters, and while many writers look at the radio people with disdain, their impact is palpable.

And yet I was spoiled, despite my odd Yankee moments. Working for what I still consider the finest paper in America, I was brought up respecting the *Times* and its contents. I did not feel that I had to go to the bizarre to get that story.

Still, I feel the pressure of change. Coaches tell me it's good to feel that you're always nervous about your assignment. Worrying about your job ensures a better performance—an essential ingredient to molding a team, claim football coaches I have known. These days, I make sure I'm at a ball game three hours before the first pitch. I listen at the lockers. I try to relate to the younger players, if not by speaking their language or humming their music, at least by showing empathy and interest for what they are. I do not want my gray hair to separate us.

When a game ends, I find myself asking a different kind of question, one that often has to do with their emotions, and maybe it makes for a better story, elicits a better response, than asking simply, "What pitch did you throw?" (Asking "breast or bottle" never seemed quite right for me.) Still, I have been caught up in daily drama myself these days. Maybe it's from watching too much television. Or maybe there's more than one way to skin a cat. But there was a certain solidity to what we in the business used to call the inverted pyramid story. You started with the most important thing and worked your way down. Now, we start with an odd event and try to figure out how not to let the score get in the way of the story.

Is all of this just a reaction—no, an overreaction—to what sportswriting was until the late 1960s? OK, so the generation that preceded me didn't call it a bat—instead it was a "wagon tongue." Who today even knows what that is? Anyone around here ever hitch a wagon to a horse? A pop fly might have been called a "dying quail," as if today's reporters had gone bird hunting. A very high fly was "a can of corn"—you know, as high as a cornstalk. Lefties forever were "southpaws," or "portsiders." A high, inside pitch that almost bopped you in the head was "chin music." The catcher's gear was called "the tools of ignorance," and third base was "the hot corner."

You would read these metaphors—clichés?—every day, after you had digested the back-page headlines that spoke of "Brooks Ink Robby" (the Dodgers signed Jackie Robinson), or "Yanks Defeat Pale Hose" (Yankees beat the White Sox). Baseball had become so cliché-ridden that when I joined the *Times,* our manual of style and usage forbid the expression "grand slam" when describing a bases-filled (never "loaded") home run (not "homer").

The tabloids had become caricatures of themselves, with their "hot corners," and "pigskin," and "wagon-tongues." Every lead seemed to be a play on words—as if the story itself could not stand on its own, but needed a clever turn of phrase. One of our older reporters, Lou Effrat, liked to refer to himself as "Kid Twist." ("Every lead I write has a twist to it," he explained.) But that "style book," as we called it at the *Times,* set a tone, delivered do's and don't's in writing a story. Indeed, it was book-length—about one hundred pages, inside hard covers. Every new copy editor at the paper received one.

Many of the words of caution I received from the copy desk weren't in the style book, but were part of *Times* tradition. It ensured—as much as anything can—that words connoting sexuality of any kind would not insinuate themselves into the old gray lady—as other newspapermen loved to call us. For example, at the *New York Times,* a horse never came from behind in the stretch. When parochial schools were competing, you'd better not write, "St. Dominic's tops St. Cecilia's," or, worse, "downs St. Cecilia's." Also, gratuitous "damn's," "butt's," and other words that could offend—even in direct quotes—were to be avoided, if not verboten. And I must admit that if you used them every other sentence, you'd either bore the reader or you were interviewing the wrong guy. But when, say, a person of some importance, who normally doesn't use profanity or language that could offend some, did in fact speak that way, then using such a word makes a telling point and is not simply gratuitous. Use it to quote Billy Martin, and you've merely wallowed in his syntax. Quote, for example, a Billie Jean King or an Arnold Palmer with a "damn" and you've got a better story with the same quote.

Over the years, as America became much more sensitive to language that could offend various groups, my paper often went overboard in making sure it would offend no one. Oh, it took a while. Billie Jean was "Mrs. King" for much of the 1970s. It was no easy time for the *Times* to turn to "Ms." Then we had another radical departure in sports when it came to identifying women. Always, when I started, a woman in a second reference was either Mrs. or Miss. Then she became Ms. Finally, even that honorific has been done away with in writing about sports figures.

Now, when we write about, say, the tennis-playing Williams sisters, we simply call them by their second name, just as we do male athletes (except, of course, when they get into trouble with the law and wind up outside the sports pages, and become "Mr."). While sportswriting in particular is freer these days at the paper, the famous "style" book is bigger than ever. When I joined the paper I was given a copy, a little red book of some 96 pages. Now it is a full-sized tome of more than 360 pages, and counting.

But the language is not without its thorns. Many years ago I wrote a piece about the Jets' aging tight end, a free-spirited fellow named Jerome Barkum. He was from Mississippi. Thus, he enjoyed feasting on typical down-home cooking. In my story, though, he pointed out that because he was getting older, he was trying to get away from foods such as, in his words, "fried chicken and pork chops." That was a direct quote. Yet my editor, Sandy Padwe, who was a gifted newspaperman, red-penciled it.

"It could sound racist," reasoned the 1960s-sensitive Padwe, who was to become a dean at the Columbia University School of Journalism.

"But he said it," I objected. "That's what he eats. He's from Mississippi."

My logical argument fell on deaf ears. Jerome Barkum was aging and watching his weight by eating more healthful foods. The reader never learned what he had cut out.

Of course, many of the nicknames in sports we used once upon a time probably were racist or stereotypical or insensitive. I think we avoided those at the paper. I never thought twice, though, of describing the exciting Montreal Canadiens hockey team as the "Flying Frenchmen." Books had been written using that name in the title. The team thought of itself that way, much as the New York Yankees were proud of the sobriquet "Bronx Bombers" (you can't say that any more). Virtually every player on the Canadiens *was* French-Canadian when I started writing about them in the 1960s.

One day, in the 1990s, after many years of not covering hockey, I did a New York Rangers–Canadiens game. Naturally, I called the Canadiens the Flying Frenchmen. At least, I tried to. One of the copy editors called me in the press box and said, "We don't describe them that way. It's a stereotype." I tried to buttress my case with a historical perspective. I lost.

In the intervening years, the Frenchmen were not the only ones who had found a sensitive ally at the *Times*. So had Gypsies. I hadn't realized they were now a protected minority. So I quoted an athlete who talked of being "gypped" by his agent. Uh, unh. No negative Gypsy connotations, I was told.

Yet I made my contribution to the language of journalism, and helped spark a debate, over the use of a word that gets into the *Times* once every twenty years. I refer, of course, to "fart."

Don't hyperventilate, gentle reader. The word never saw print in my paper. At least not in my story. I wish it would have. It was, in fact, the crux of the story. I will explain:

The Jets had just lost a game in the Seattle Kingdome on Monday Night Football when punter Chuck Ramsey messed up a punt. I dashed down to the locker room at game's end, and collared Ramsey. He was crying.

"What is it—that punt, Chuck?" I asked. "You're pretty upset."

"How would you feel," he asked, "if your coach told you, in front of the entire team, 'I can fart farther than you can punt?'"

I made one of the great efforts of my life not to laugh. But I had to be serious. Chuck was really upset. Who could blame him? Coach Walt Michaels was one of the most honest people I had known. He was one of the most accessible coaches also. I confess: I loved being around the big lug. I enjoyed hearing his stories of working in the Pennsylvania coal mines, of listening to morals he brought to Polish fables that his father, from the old country, had told him. Above Walt's desk was a portrait of his father done by a family friend. Underneath it was the inscription, "Glad he made the boat."

Jets punter Chuck Ramsey. Courtesy of the New York Jets.

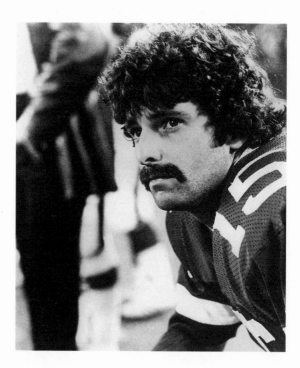

In Walt's very basic world, there were no excuses. He enjoyed telling the story of the Polish sea captain who went through a terrible storm. The owner of the boat told him later, "Don't tell me if the sea was stormy. Did you bring my boat in?"

Yes, Walt was crude, too. So . . . "fart." How to handle this indelicate word in the delicate world of the *New York Times*? We recently had been advised by our assistant managing editor and protector of the written word, Allan M. Siegal, that if we really felt a bad word belonged in a story, to consult with the copy editors first. He also said that we were not to alter the word if it were not used, but instead would use an ellipsis, or three dots, to indicate the word had been removed. Or we might bracket a different word to show this was the meaning, if not the actual word. None of my pleadings made an impression on the copy desk. I was told I couldn't use the word, but to soften the quote. In other words, I was to change the word.

This I did. Thus, Michaels's outburst came out as "I can spit farther than you can punt."

When I returned to New York the next day, I got my hands on all the other papers to see how their erudite desks handled this sensitive matter. One paper simply put a dash where the "fart" had been. Another avoided the quote. But *Newsday,* the big Long Island paper, to its credit actually used the quote accurately. In Monday's paper, at any rate. When I picked up *Newsday* on Tuesday, I discovered it had now bracketed the word and replaced it with another in a follow-up story.

This caught the eye of *Newsday*'s media critic, who had a Sunday column. He wrote an entire piece about how the New York media had handled the word "fart"—which I'm sure was a first in the history of sports journalism in America. He noted how *Newsday* alone had accurately used the word in its Monday story, but then backed off a day later. And how the *Times* had changed the word to "spit." When he called Siegal and asked about altering the quote, Siegal told him that was against *Times* policy and would not happen in the future.

In a way, I felt vindicated, but still I was left without a "fart" among the millions of words in my clips.

I wonder what the courtly longtime publisher, Arthur Hays Sulzberger, would have said to that word. He steered the paper from 1935 to

1961. We met when I had a summer job in 1954, just before I started college.

I had never actually *seen* Mr. Sulzberger. I delivered notes or other unimportant bits of information from my clerical job in the accounting department. When I actually had something for Sulzberger himself, I would take the elevator up to the fourteenth floor, walk what seemed to be half a mile down the red carpet, and hand it to a little old lady who came out of Central Casting—gray hair in a bun, somewhat forbidding, quite Victorian. Mr. Sulzberger's secretary.

Before going back to school, I wanted a souvenir of my stay at the paper. I bought a recently published history of the *Times* at the remaindered price of one dollar, and, enclosing a note, sent it up to Mr. Sulzberger himself and asked if he would autograph it. The next day, for a reason I still can't remember—perhaps it was the end of summer, and I didn't need to worry about looking so Timesian—I decided to dress down for the job. Rather than wear a white shirt and tie, I sported a purple Hawaiian sunburst shirt.

The phone rang at my desk. It was the little old lady with the gray hair. "Can you come up here?" she asked. "Mr. Sulzberger would like to see you."

I hesitated a second, looking for an excuse not to go up in the outfit I was wearing. But I chanced it, and went upstairs.

The secretary ushered me into Sulzberger's office. He was an imposing figure in his oak-paneled room, behind his big desk, his nearby autographed photos of presidents. He had a desk filled with mementos from heads of state, who visited the paper on their trips to New York. He was a handsome, white-haired patrician and he had an engaging smile.

"So what are your plans?" he asked me.

I told him I was starting college in a few days, and hoped to become a newspaperman.

He picked up the book I had sent him. "I've autographed it for you, and I want it to be my gift to you. So I'm enclosing a check for the purchase price," he said.

I looked at the inscription. It read, "To Gerald Eskenazi, with the hope that his interest in The New York Times will continue for many years to

**Arthur Hays Sulzberger,
longtime publisher of
the *New York Times.***
Photo courtesy of the
New York Times.

come." Alongside it was Mr. Sulzberger's personal check for five dollars—the book's list price.

"But I only paid a dollar for it," I said, stupidly. I guess I figured that
at this seminal moment in my life, I should be scrupulously honest.

"Oh, don't worry about it, we'll take care of it," he said, as he led me to
his secretary's desk.

After he went back into his office, I explained to her that I had only
paid a dollar for the book. She said they'd send me another check for the
correct amount. I handed her back the five-dollar check.

The next day, I got the one-dollar check in the office mail. I pasted it
inside the book. A few weeks later, I got a call from the office of Amory
Bradford, the paper's chief financial officer.

"Mr. Bradford has been trying to balance Mr. Sulzberger's personal
checking account, but there is a check outstanding for one dollar," Bradford's secretary told me.

"But I wanted to keep it as a souvenir," I said.

"OK, bring it in and we'll photocopy it for you, then you can cash it," she said.

It was the least I could do. I could just imagine Mr. Sulzberger, meeting with the Italian ambassador or receiving the Japanese emperor, distracted over his one-dollar uncashed check.

So I brought the check in, got it copied, and then cashed it. The book, with the copy of that one-dollar check, remains in my office, fifty years after I put the two together. Mr. Sulzberger was prescient. My interest in the *New York Times* in fact continued for "many years to come."

9

The Press of a Button

I believe the exponential rise of cable television with its four major all-news-all-the-time channels, along with the popularity of the anything-goes talks shows and the so-called reality series that are pumping advertising dollars into the networks, have created a very different type of newspaper—and thus, a very different type of newspaper story.

Just days before the events of 9/11 altered America's perception of itself and the way it goes about its daily business, Howell Raines became the *Times*'s new executive editor—the most important voice about what goes on in the news pages and how that news is delivered. Soon, he did not refer to "stories," but to "our daily news report." I started seeing that expression increasingly, used by the publisher, other editors, and spokespersons as well. There is a good reason for this "daily news report"—if you say that, then you are talking about something besides a newspaper story. Use the words "newspaper story" and you exclude the Internet. Or television. And the *Times* wants itself to be seen—and I believe it is succeeding—as a brand name that delivers something more than a newspaper. Indeed, it now has a television arm, and is coproducing shows based on investigative stories it has done. It is also, or wants to be, something besides "The New York" *Times*. Its national edition is filled with major-college sports events, often to the exclusion of New York–oriented teams. Even some of the editorials, if they are purely local in nature, are excluded from the national edition. And now the *International Herald*

Tribune is exclusively a New York Times property, after the *Times* bought out its partner, the *Washington Post*. Europeans may want more soccer or cricket than pieces about the Knicks, Nets, or Islanders.

This new environment of news-gathering and of then making the "daily report" has turned us all into show-business acolytes. I see this at its highest level at the annual show known as the Super Bowl.

It is at once the easiest and most difficult event to write about. You spend a season with, and writing about, a football team. And then at the end, after five thousand words a week for more than twenty weeks, you wind up pulling your hair, hyperventilating and rushing to write within an hour or two about an event of such huge appeal that it is annually America's highest-rated television show, attracting half the country. I had never seen anything like the organization of a Super Bowl week, and after more than twenty times of being immersed in this frenzy of writing and reporting I still haven't seen its equal at an Olympics (summer or winter), a World Series, a Stanley Cup championship, or a heavyweight title fight.

My favorite Super Bowl photo is black-and-white. Six reporters, wearing jackets and ties, are sitting at poolside in Miami, surrounding Joe Namath, who is in a lounge chair. They are all scribbling notes while he is in his bathing suit looking serene. That was Super Bowl III.

Go to a Super Bowl as a member of the news media these days and you will find yourself part of a choreographed environment worthy of a Rockettes' performance, or a military maneuver. Hotels swarm with uniformed and plainclothes police. Autograph seekers are rousted out of the lobby, or kept behind a rope. Reporters can't even register at the team hotels (unless, and only with some teams, they are from the club's hometown).

If you're a member of the news media, and you're lucky, you can get through to a player's room by telephone, or you might talk to an athlete if he is willing to see you after hours. Essentially, though, the media schedule is precise and restrictive, and I have become part of a herd. We all receive an eight-page folder describing the routine: interviews start on Sunday nights with both teams upon arrival, when the head coach and six players are available for half an hour at their respective hotels. The schedule is repeated on Monday night.

Then there is the mammoth Media Day on Tuesday, an undertaking so huge it can be held only at the stadium because more than three thousand members of the media show up. That's right—a mix of three thousand reporters, television camera crews, radio announcers, TV sideline correspondents. They're all there. When we start to stream out of the tunnels and into the stands, where the players are waiting for us in carefully assigned spots, the sight alone scares some of the players. I have seen more than a few taken by surprise, as if they expected to be trampled. Other players have a sense of humor about the mass interrogation and bring along their own video cameras. So they are taping us while we are taping them.

The team's key players are given podiums on the field below, but up in the stands players are sitting, surrounded by reporters. Some trip over stairs, after banging into boom microphones or being jostled by other reporters. This goes on for an hour. The team goes back to its hotel, the media has breakfast, and then the other team arrives and the inquisition starts anew.

It was at one of these media days, for Super Bowl XXII, that the Washington Redskins' Doug Williams was asked the famed question, "How long have you been a black quarterback?" That question has become a symbol of stupid Super Bowl questions. It came during the week that Williams was going to be the first black quarterback to start a Super Bowl game. The funny thing is, I intended to ask that question, tongue-in-cheek, hoping to elicit a response by Williams that seemed to me quite important. The dwelling by my colleagues on his race had, I felt, trivialized his accomplishments, and I wondered how he felt about that. In other words, had he turned suddenly into a black quarterback just this week?

I never got to ask the question—luckily for me, it turns out—and the fellow who did became a laughingstock, a poster-boy for stupid Super Bowl questioning. I hope he asked it in the same spirit I had planned to. If so, then no one else got it but us.

There are more mass conferences the rest of the week, but these are held at the team hotels, usually in a ballroom. Each player is assigned a table with his name on it. You pull up a chair and sit down and talk to him.

You have been in the Super Bowl city for almost a week, and have not seen one lick of football. This is the world's only sporting event in which nobody can watch practice. Well, there are one or two reporters—embedded "pool" reporters for each team. The two writers file daily reports about practice, but they are not allowed to write about what they've seen—merely trivia such as who practiced, and a player's or coach's comments. So no one knows about surprises one team may have, and no one knows how the punter has been kicking the ball or whether a key player has recovered from his injury.

Some coaches are like this all year round. While I was fascinated by the machinations of Bill Parcells when he took over as Jets' coach and team puppeteer, I also was distressed by his refusal to let us watch practice once training camp ended. So I for one was accustomed to not seeing clubs work out during Super Bowl week. That didn't mean I had to like it. For Super Bowl week, you're writing endless speculation.

On Friday, there would be more orchestrated reporting: the so-called State-of-the-NFL address by the commissioner, an often somber hour in which he will make an announcement about important future plans, or respond to a planted question by a favored member of the media. Before this heavily attended performance—you need the ballroom of the headquarters hotel to fit in everyone—the commissioner privately goes through a mock news conference with several staff members, who quiz him on likely difficult questions. Thus, he has a surprising lode of information at his fingertips when the real press conference starts. Invariably, every newspaper covering the event will have a story about the commissioner the next day, in addition to the incredible array of football pieces, graphics, and photographs.

Actually, all of this is pretty easily written. The game is the pain.

On a "morning" paper such as the *Times,* with deadlines that can give you facial tics, the Super Bowl game story has evolved into a series of deadline nightmares, fifteen hundred words (the equivalent of seven typewritten pages) written while my eyes dart between the game and the computer screen. I have written as many as four complete Super Bowl stories in one afternoon and evening.

Our national edition goes in at 9 P.M.—and the game is just about half over by then. So that means I've had to write an "early" story. It will not be about anything that happens in the game, because when this paper goes to press, the game has not yet ended. So I try to write about a compelling aspect leading up to the game—say, rehashing the Doug Williams story and its significance. Or at another game I wrote about the 49ers and their place in history.

But then comes the difficult piece—the "running" story. This is for the edition with an 11 P.M. deadline—lots of fun, because the Super Bowl is over at about 10:15.

I will keep some of the copy from my early story for this one, because it is, frankly, brutal to write a story as the game is being played. You put some significance into a sentence about a play you've just witnessed, and then, suddenly, something else has happened that is even more important. I try to wait until half-time, which lasts about thirty minutes and affords me a decent amount of time to put at least the first half of the game into perspective. I can write about seven hundred words in that time frame. Add another three hundred from my earlier story, and I've already got a thousand words.

Now, a game ending forty-five minutes before deadline doesn't seem so bad. When the last whistle has blown, I start my story from the top, trying to pick up some other aspect of the game which wasn't mentioned exactly the same way in my "running account." I write about four hundred freshly minted words. Use a clever transitional phrase, and I'm able to "pick up" my early copy—seamlessly, I hope.

It doesn't end there, though. Now I've got to write a final piece—using quotes, anecdotes, statistics that weren't available to me the moment the game ended, or facts such as the game's MVP or records set. And I've also got a better perspective, having finally caught my breath.

Here is how I started my piece on Williams's Super Bowl in 1988:

"Doug Williams turned Super Bowl XXII into a record-setting offensive show today, as well as a historic event, by throwing four second-quarter touchdown passes in the Washington Redskins' 42–10 victory over the Denver Broncos."

I'm proud of that lead because I was able to put some historical perspective into it, while also getting the relevant football facts. Maybe, on reflection, it was somewhat long, but then again, this was an important moment. And always, in the back of my mind, was that I was writing for a paper that prides itself on being a record-keeper. It's comforting to know that every story that appears will also be preserved on micro-film—and today, on-line.

What bothers me, though, about this endless production on Super Bowl Sunday is that, first of all, I don't get to really see the game. I don't mean as a fan, but as a reporter. It's hard to discern shifts of momen-tum, or team emotion, or crowd reaction in this buzz-saw of writing ac-tivity. And the Super Bowl also does not afford you the chance, if you're writing the lead story about the game, to go to the locker rooms and see the players' reactions to what has just taken place. Instead, you sit in the press box, watch the most valuable player interviewed on the television sets that are placed strategically throughout the box, digest the literally dozens of pages of player quotes, team statistics (including game-time temperature and wind velocity, even in indoor stadiums), and lists of records set.

Over many years, I have fielded many questions from people I meet who wonder: "Do you actually go to the games? Or do you write them off the television." Well, when it comes to the Super Bowl, the answer is "yes" to both. Here is the irony of writing about a Super Bowl game: it's probably the biggest event of the year you will cover, and it has the worst conditions for writing. That is why, I believe, there has never been an award for the best Super Bowl game story handed out in various writing competitions.

This problem led me to suggest a radical change in how we report it. After watching a few Super Bowls from the luxury of the press box as the sidebar writer, I suggested to my editor, Joe Vecchione, that we use two people to write the game story: One would write the "running," while the other would take it all in, take appropriate notes, and at the end of the game be refreshed and have a perspective to be able to write a final story. Joe agreed to this rather unusual idea. And so in one Super Bowl I wrote the running story, and Mike Janofsky, who was our NFL-at-large writer, watched the game. When it ended, he put everything to-gether, with the luxury of perspective, and I dashed down to the locker rooms to do a sidebar. If you picked up various editions the next day, you'd see my story of the game in one, and then Mike's in another. But it worked.

It's no piece of cake writing the sidebars, though. About fifteen minutes before the end of the game, reporters who want to go to the locker
room are ushered there by members of the league's, or teams', public relations staff. You need a guide because often you are traversing places in
an unfamiliar stadium, negotiating your way past hordes of fans. The
p.r. assistants, though, have practiced this routine during the week, actually having taken dry runs to the locker rooms and interview areas.
They rarely get lost (although that has happened). That is the easy way
to go. But if you wait until the end of the game, then you have to make
your way through a madhouse by yourself, past fans, yelling and screaming, waving arms, singing. How do you do this? You follow color-coded
arrows, painted on the floor, all the way downstairs.

To leave or not to leave before the game is over? There is no easy way
to get it just right. Invariably, I wait until a game is over. There's just
something about seeing the crowd reaction, and the players and the
coaches, that I believe helps you in your story. And in Super Bowl XXV,
which the Giants won, I could not leave until the end because I was
watching the skies. My assignment that game was security because of
the Gulf War. While everyone in the place was watching Scott Nor-
wood's missed field-goal attempt for the Buffalo Bills in the final minute, I was looking at the U.S. military helicopter circling above the
stadium.

But when the Bengals and 49ers were playing Super Bowl XXIII in
1989, my assignment was to interview the winning quarterback. The
Bengals were leading a close game, but I chose to follow the crowd of
writers and went down to the assigned interview area. By the time I got
there, the game still was on, and television monitors were set up for us
to view the action. At this point, Boomer Esiason of the Bengals was the
one we figured was going to step onto the podium to talk to us. I already
had voted for the game's most valuable player, and it was a Bengal. But
in the bowels of the stadium, cramped, pressed against other writers,
not even seeing the climactic moment in person, I watched Joe Montana throw a touchdown pass to John Taylor that gave San Francisco the
victory.

People who were left in the press box had to change their ballots for
the MVP voting, the people from Disney World had to invite a 49er

instead of a Bengal, and there were other last-second shifts. But I was glad, despite the pandemonium downstairs, that I didn't have to write the game story. Everything that had come before was virtually superfluous to the drama of the climax.

I've got to hand it to Boomer, whom I got to know much better a few years later when he became a Jet. This was a devastating moment in his career, yet he handled it graciously. He even struck an ironic note: "There I was on the sideline, rehearsing my 'I'm going to Disney World' speech, when Montana threw the touchdown," Esiason quipped. Speaking of grace under pressure.

I believe the Super Bowl has only one other near equivalent in sports— a heavyweight championship fight—that gets a writer's juices flowing. Each decides a title—as opposed to, say, the start of a World Series, or NBA championship, or Stanley Cup final, or the NCAA's Final Four. Although I had been in the business for thirty-five years, and had written my share of fights, boxing had not been my beat. Then one day I was asked how I'd feel about covering boxing.

Nothing in life, or professionally, prepares you for covering the fights— I mean, unless you've had an abnormal life. Suddenly, I entered a world of gladiators and hustlers, gamblers and tycoons. There were ex-felons, and soon-to-be felons, and always, the raw brutality of the ring itself. And I loved all of it. I told my wife, "This is like being around some of the people I grew up with in Brooklyn—the ones that didn't go straight."

To a fan, or a newspaper reader or television viewer, boxing appears to be the most elemental sport of them all, so simple to write about, and yet it stunned and delighted me with one surprise after the other. I don't mean the pounding in the ring—although unless you're at a fight in person, you don't really catch the basic brutality and courage of these guys. There is a world of difference in seeing blood spurting out of a cut on television—or splotching onto your computer and your shirt. It happens, and it's red.

I enjoyed, first of all, the people surrounding the fighters. They take up much of your time if you're a reporter. The fights themselves last less than an hour, and indeed can be over in fewer than three minutes.

Every fight has a hype-factor, and this is where your ability to handle the truth comes in. Alas, you're dealing with characters for whom truth is so precious, they use it sparingly.

These were my buddies: I had a convivial dinner one night in Vegas with one of the boxing people, a manager. He had gray hair, which he wore in a ponytail, as certain men in their fifties are wont to do. He was a fellow Brooklynite, but the subject of the South came up, and he started to talk about Atlanta.

"I was there in federal prison," he said.

"What did you do?" I asked, thinking he had committed a white-collar crime.

"You don't want to know," he said mysteriously.

What do you say to someone at a moment like that? What would my friends and neighbors, many of them doctors and lawyers, in the sub-urbs of Long Island say if they were having dinner with someone, and that subject came up? That was another moment, I was sure, few people out of my business ever would know.

In the days leading up to a big fight, stories write themselves. Pro-moters these days have themes—perhaps a take-off on Ali's own "Rumble in the Jungle" of Zaire, or his "Thrilla in Manila," against Frazier. Some-times, fighters themselves bring up an issue—such as South Africa's Frans Botha, who liked to say, "I'm white, but I can fight."

Riddick Bowe, who, like Tyson, was from my old neighborhood, liked to think of himself as a family man. He paraded his family in front of the immediate world. His wife, Judy, and their children used to come to training camp and watch him spar. The youngsters, barely out of their toddler years, would sit in their mother's lap and gawk up at the ring while he was pummeling a sparring partner. After one such session, we talked about his life in Brooklyn. He had gone to my old high school, Thomas Jefferson.

"You grew up around the corner from my house," I told him.

"Yeah, but you weren't there any more when I lived there," he said. "All the Jews moved out of the neighborhood. It wasn't good enough for them."

"Oh," I replied. "You still live there, Riddick?"

Sheepishly, he said, "Well, no."

"Well, no," was exactly right. He was building a multi-million-dollar home in a Washington suburb.

Bowe was to be a figure in another bizarre chapter in the education of a sportswriter, and it was further proof that a journalist can deliver the story no matter what the working conditions, or whatever happens to fall from the sky.

At first, the story was of a good, old-fashioned heavyweight title fight— Bowe against the redoubtable Evander Holyfield, the Bible-spouting physical fitness freak who, perhaps, listened too closely to the admonition to "be fruitful and multiply." Evander had several children out of wedlock, while remaining married to another.

The bout, at Caesars Palace, attracted the usual parade of fight characters: women whose buttocks were visible through a see-through window of their plastic hot pants; real and would-be pimps in Three Musketeers purple feathered hats; semi- or once-famous Hollywood types, and entourages from the likes of Donald Trump, or Steve Wynn, or the sister of the late Nicole Simpson or the army of lawyers who had defended O. J.

I already had written my thirteen-hundred-word early story for the national edition and settled in at ringside. I was munching on some pretzels when someone tapped me on the shoulder.

"Can I have some?" he asked. It was Reggie Jackson.

"Want any mustard for them?" I joked, reminding him of his "hot dog" nickname. He wagged a finger at me.

My running story was going along smoothly, with the preliminary-fight paragraphs out of the way, the "color" aspects of my main piece already worked through (it's easy to write a fight crowd; they actually write the story for you). Now I was doing the "running," and my fingers were hitting the keys with the rapidity of punches. For you have only one minute between rounds to summarize what has happened. If you wait too long to compose your thoughts, you're already into the next round, you've lost your train of thought, and then your head gets woozy as if someone had nailed you with a right.

Still, I had gotten used to this sort of deadline pressure, even looked forward to seeing how quickly and well I could write under pressure, what new adjectives I could concoct for a left hook or the way a fighter moved his head or to capture the expression on his face. Even when I was the paper's hockey maven, and odd-sports editor, as I liked to describe myself after stints at Irish hurling or dog shows, and then describing pro football, I always wondered what I could do as the boxing writer. I wanted to show my stuff. Boxing was pure description.

Now, as I was hitting the keys on my computer, I had a strange sensation as if something was sailing down toward ringside from the sky. But that's absurd, I thought. For the moment, I had become disoriented. Because of the glare of the overhead ring lights, all I could see was blackness above me, so I had imagined I was in an indoor ring instead of Caesars outdoors theater.

And then I saw a man on a motorized kite-like contraption heading straight for me on the other side of the ring. I instinctively ducked. When nothing happened, I looked up and saw he was tangled in the ropes. Everyone was screeching and people were hitting him on the head with cell phones. They kept whacking away until he was knocked unconscious. Alongside him, the Reverend Jesse Jackson cringed in horror, while a few seats away, Judy Bowe, six months pregnant, was screaming.

It took almost half an hour to sort things out. The flyer was a publicity nut who nicknamed himself the Fan Man, and had jumped out of a private plane, hoping to land in the ring with his whirring, fan-driven contraption. He nearly made it. But when he swooped down, he clipped the top of Reverend Jackson's head, and then got tangled in the ropes. One of Jackson's bodyguards, not knowing what was going on, immediately started to swat the Fan Man. So did various boxing people. They always carry some sort of weapon. I mean, you never know.

Before the fight could continue—and it did continue—Judy Bowe fainted, and Eddie Futch, Bowe's eighty-year-old trainer, had heart palpitations and had to leave, too.

When the fight ended, I ran up to Jesse Jackson and introduced myself. I asked him his reaction to what happened, and he said he could understand the man being beaten up because no one knew what his intentions were. One of Jackson's associates told me, "We thought they were trying to assassinate Jesse."

Again, this was one of those stories that required a multifaceted lead. For in addition to the remarkable occurrence that involved Jackson, one of the country's iconic figures, Holyfield had done something very unusual in the history of prizefighting—regain a heavyweight championship. One thought alone couldn't deal with the situation adequately—even though a single thought in the lead was always what they had told you in journalism class. But that was before sports got complicated.

So, my story in the *Times* of November 7, 1993, began this way:

"Evander Holyfield survived history, a younger, bigger opponent, and a bizarre delay after a parachutist landed in the ropes in a fight he was dominating, to regain his heavyweight title tonight from Riddick Bowe."

Well, Bowe recovered from that beating and eventually came back to reclaim his title. But when I last read about him, ten years later, he was preparing to serve jail time for kidnapping his wife, Judy, and their children. I don't think he was trying to bring them back to Brooklyn.

The big fights will earn millions for each combatant these days, but there was also a nickel-and-dime aspect to the fight game that intrigued me. Most of the fighters worked out in gyms that transported me into another time, almost a surreal world.

I remember one of them in Brooklyn. I walked up a flight of stairs, opened the heavy metal door, and the scene flickered, like slow motion from an old black-and-white movie: someone was hitting the heavy bag, off in a corner a man in shorts was skipping rope before a mirror, and in the ring, two fighters stalked and jabbed.

For a couple of bucks and a dream, one man could hit another. These gyms, these fighters, which still are strewn throughout the country (only the big-money boys can afford well-tended fight camps in the mountains) are throwbacks to an era of cigar smoke, when fighters were named Rocky or Izzy, when promoters were called Mushky.

In one of the broken-down gyms I met a former champion named Harold Weston. He understood what a gym means to someone harboring a dream. "I hope the gyms stay in business," said Weston. "There was one over on West 28th Street, I paid to keep it going. When it went out, some kids got in trouble, some got killed, some went back to the streets."

I visited another, barely out of the shadow of the Brooklyn Bridge. There I had one of those encounters that made me glad I had become a sportswriter. My accountant friends Murray or Hal could never tell such good stories.

At the top of the stairs, there was a poster with a paean to boxing from the Roman poet Virgil: "Now, whoever has courage and a strong and collected spirit in his breast let him come forward, lace on the gloves and put up his hands." The owner of the gym told me that one of the gym habitués had asked about the author. "Is that Virgil Hill from Brooklyn?" asked the fighter. "I didn't know he could talk like that."

If you want to know who the people were in my new world of covering boxing, this conversation I had with a gym owner might explain everything:

"This is the last melting pot in New York," he explained. "We've got criminals, narc agents, people who come in here with no intention to spar. But it's a natural progression. You come in, you want to test yourself." That included lawyers from the nearby courthouse.

I also met an amateur fighter named Kangaroo Jackson, and another who wore a shirt that proclaimed himself "The Renegade Jew."

"That's me," said a forty-six-year-old fellow named David Lawrence. "I take fights for $400. You know what it costs me to fight for $400? I lose $3,000. I bring all my friends. I've flown them to Boston, to Colorado." Lawrence claimed to have a Ph.D. in literature from Columbia.

At a gym in Times Square I ran across a proprietor who said his mother was descended from nobility in Nigeria. He was upset over his son, whom he had raised to be a middleweight.

"Instead, he became a vegetarian."

One man told he had just finished sparring with a woman. "She was tough," he said.

On the wall there was an old movie poster of the British Marilyn Monroe knockoff, Diana Dors ("Half-Angel Half-Devil, She Made Him Half-Man"), that vied with another poster: "No spitting."

Ah, spitting. You've got to have a bit of a stomach if you're going to be a boxing writer. At the first weigh-in I covered, I saw something I had never read about, and hadn't been aware that boxers went through.

One of the fighters had come in over the limit for his weight class. He took off his shorts to step on the scale (someone held a towel in front of him), but he still was too heavy. He had to lose some ounces to qualify.

So he began to spit.

"What's he doing?" I asked my friend Katz. "What does it look like?" Mike replied. "He's trying to lose weight."

And so every fifteen or twenty seconds, after summoning up more saliva and then making a pucker motion with his lips to roll it around, the boxer spit into a paper cup. He did this for an hour, taking a break to force himself to urinate, then went back on the scales.

He had done it. Then someone handed him two milk-carton-sized bottles of water, and he began to drink. He had to avoid dehydration. Of course, not only had I never realized what some boxers go through to make the weight, I also was fascinated and troubled by this scene. Some fighters, I learned, bloated themselves after making the weight so they could actually come in much heavier. Some actually gained seven or eight pounds in a day, and so they had a considerable weight advantage over their opponents. Once they had officially "made the weight," they didn't have to go on the scales again.

Then again, some fighters were given the benefit of a pound or two by a helpful trainer or manager. It was amusing to see one handler help his fighter by sticking a toe on the scale when the opponent stepped on it— making him overweight, and forcing him to go through the spitting routine.

After watching an afternoon of these shenanigans, writing the actual fight is easy (except, of course, when someone nearly parachutes in your lap).

But my surprises in this business hardly were limited to the fight game. For in the midst of my foray into boxing, I went to Norway to write about the Winter Olympics. I had done previous Olympics, in Lake Placid and the French Alps, and had been in Barcelona for the summer games as well. Now, though, the Olympics had become an all-out television show, with its high-tech gadgetry, its schedules informed by considerations of Nielsen ratings in the States. The television brain trust had learned long ago that figure skating was the highest-rated Olympic sport—and the one sport guaranteed to get out the women viewers.

In my business, you learn to ask questions of people who know. Before every Olympics the *Times* does a huge pullout section that describes these quadrennial sports and explains how they are judged. I would write stories for this section about something I had never seen. How many people grew up knowing anything about the biathlon, that combination of cross-country skiing and rifle marksmanship? There wasn't much chance of my seeing this in Brooklyn—or competing in luge, or even figure skating.

I learned very quickly in the newspaper business that people are eager to answer the phone and talk to a reporter if you're calling about something of a positive nature, or if you can get their name in the paper and it's not because of a rape or arson. Thus, my Winter Olympics expertise. Writing about sports I had never seen taught me that I could trust my instincts. The first time I saw Mary Lou Retton bound onto the mats at Madison Square Garden I didn't have to know how to judge a gymnastics event to realize she was something special. The great ones make it easy for sportswriters. If you have any understanding of sports at all, you can tell who's the best—even in a sport you've never seen before. I found this to be true in figure skating as well, even though it is a sport that taxes judges' knowledge because of the intricacies of movement. But the first time I saw another champion on the ice, Gordie Howe, I understood why he was considered hockey's finest player. There are some athletes, even in the whirl of a team sport, who instantly make themselves distinctive.

Now, when I was writing about athletes and sports I had no real in-depth knowledge about, I found that describing what they do—not just stating it as fact—enhanced my expertise in the readers' mind. I also learned to throw in some technical terms—a "camel" in figure-skating, a "trick" in gymnastics, a "schuss-boom" in skiing—and for the next morning's reader, I was a veritable scholar, an insider in the jock-ocracy.

When I went off to the Alps, the *Times* had allowed us to spend as much money as we needed on winter clothing. That was quite different from the time I went to Lake Placid in 1980, when someone in the paper's accounting department had bought a bunch of moon boots and big parkas wholesale, and handed them out. When the Lake Placid games were over, we had to return the winter gear to the paper, which I'm told sold them to some used-clothing company. That was very un-*Times*ian. I'm glad the paper got out of the used-clothing business.

So I was covered from head to toe with first-rate gear in Norway when I took the bus from the press headquarters up to the mountains for some ski-jumping. I also had a clipping from the paper explaining ski-jumping. I read it on the way up.

It was a breathtaking scene when I got there. I stood just beneath a pristine white peak, the air snapping cold, the spectators lining up along the jump-line, their pink faces topped by colorful knit hats.

In ski-jumping, there is a long moment when the competitor is lost from view—the jumper is dipping downhill for momentum, then turns into an aerodynamic creature and soars a few hundred feet before landing. The Olympic Games did something nice for the spectators—but it was one of the more incongruous scenes I had witnessed. For high on the mountain, this pristine rock, there was a Jumbotron television screen—that's right, television so the fans who were standing there and watching the event, and who momentarily lost sight of the jumping athlete, could witness him or her from start to finish.

Outdoor television in this environment! I realized that this was still another instance of people not satisfied any longer to believe their eyes. The panorama of the event, the ambience, all of it had to be defined by what could fit on the television screen. It hit home once more: people needed their sensibilities stimulated to enhance what they were watching, even in person. Imagine the difficulty we in the newspaper business now have to catch their attention when they are sitting still with a folded paper in their hands. We were a cold medium. Marshall McLuhan once had correctly described television as a "hot medium," but I don't think he realized how that pervaded people's lives outside of their living room.

I thought of this instant feed to viewers as I watched the Iraqi conflict unfold in 2003. We were not watching a war so much as a series of vignettes—something like a play-by-play of a ball game. Except that this was taken from the narrowest of perspectives—wherever there happened to be a camera, or a reporter. So if at that moment you happened to turn on the television and there was an incoming round and the reporter was scared to death, that is the image that traveled across the United States, if not the world. And if we happened to capture fourteen troops while the cameras were rolling, why, then, it looked as if we were rolling toward Baghdad unimpeded.

Technology had become king, rather than a human voice putting everything into perspective.

Naturally, I had seen these giant screens at ballparks for years. The first ones were known as DiamondVision (not because they were at baseball diamonds, but because they were made by Mitsubishi, whose logo consists of diamonds). In baseball, their function really had more to do with advertising, or promotions. Then, of course, they became the rage at football games, where you really need replay. Except for a player catching a pass, most plays occur in a crowd and are difficult to see. So now, the fans in the stands had the same benefits as the viewers at home.

I guess it wasn't much of a stretch to bring the big screens to the great outdoors—or cameras sending back images from the battlefront in real-time. So when I covered the luge events (those snaking sleds hurtling down an enclosed course), or the bobsleds, or skiing, I saw the screens everywhere. Fans no longer were content to see a luger whoosh by them—the fan had to see where he had just come from, and where he was going. The fan, and by extension the viewer at home, now needs 360 degrees of reality. He needs it horizontally, vertically. And if he doesn't get it, he feels he has missed something.

I have also had significant moments with events that needed a small space.

Now, I don't claim to have been responsible for making the case for the so-called Ping-Pong diplomacy initiative that helped define (in a good way) President Nixon's tenure. But I was there early on. By the way, in those days of the early 1970s, the *Times* never called a ping-pong tournament a ping-pong tournament. It was, technically, a table-tennis tournament. The name Ping-Pong, you see, was a trademark name of Parker Brothers, the games people. In the same way, we never used to describe people jumping on a Trampoline (another trademark). We would call it by its generic name—a rebound-tumbler. I doubt most readers knew what we were talking about.

In any event, I got a tip from the office of the Nassau county executive that an official from Mainland China was going to be visiting Long Island to help launch the first U.S. foray into Ping-Pong diplomacy. A tournament between Chinese and Americans was to be held at Long Island's big indoor arena, the Nassau Coliseum, where the Islanders hockey team and Nets basketball team played. The county executive, a career politician named Ralph Caso, was enjoying some local celebrity status because of the coliseum. It helped give Long Island a national identity beyond being known for Jones Beach and the Hamptons. So Caso's p.r. guy called me and invited me to go along for the ride as Caso picked up the Chinese big-wig at the airport.

While this event may have been lost to sports fans in the decades since, I had the feeling it was going to be very significant. For it was the first time in almost twenty-five years that an official from China was welcomed to an event in the States. When he was ushered into Caso's limo, the official greeted me warmly.

"Ah, *New York Times*," he said, the only English words he would utter the whole trip. His interpreter fielded my questions, and I had a high old time making like a foreign correspondent. Meanwhile, Caso, who I assume never had taken a course in using proper body language in front of Asians, sat with his legs crossed, exposing the soles of his shoes. I knew enough to keep my feet planted on the floor of the car, as did our Chinese guest.

Although it was to take decades before there was anything like normalization between our two countries, I had been there at the beginning of the first feelers. Did my positive-spin writing about the talents of the Chinese table-tennis stars push this along? Well, no one from the State Department ever called me to complain. Maybe there is something to the Olympics ideal and the concept that athletics breaks down barriers.

One thing I realized in writing about these non-mainstream sports: the competitors take them very seriously. So I learned to respect—or at least, show respect for—some of these odd games, or contests that most fans had never seen. Indeed, I suspect the majority of Americans barely are aware there are such contests.

Take the Unites States Dart Championships, for example. Yes, that's right—dart championship. I don't recall how or why we covered it. I don't believe we had done it before, or since. But some enterprising fellow who ran a sporting-goods store somewhere in Greenwich Village sponsored the event, it titillated one of our editors, and—voilà—there I was.

I always thought that to win at darts you simply had to toss bull's-eyes. Well, I soon learned it's about points, and you have to produce exactly a given point total to win. So while a "bull" (as the dartists term a bull's-eye) is nice, it is as difficult to hit the narrow red or green strips circling the board and that have different point values. I now know what a "double-top" is, a fact I have never used again until now. I even found out that the board is made of boar's bristles, which close tightly together after the dart has been removed.

But the dartists were very serious on one point: they didn't like anyone to make fun of their sport. Let's face it, except for seeing dart boards in someone's basement, the one place almost all of us have seen a board is in a bar. So I fought my desire to write about drinking and darting. It was almost impossible. One of the competitors actually threw darts with his right hand while holding an unopened bottle of beer in his left.

"It's the way I'm used to doing it," he explained.

When my story came out the next day, the promoter, who owned a darts store, called me. "It's the best story on darts I've ever read," he said.

When I tell that anecdote to people, they invariably add, "Yeah, and probably the only one, too."

And yet, these small stories were critical to my career. They proved a way to show what I could do when I had been a copy boy (besides getting the coffee order right). When I began at the *Times*, we used to run stories about Sunday church sermons in the Monday paper. They were pieces of about two hundred words, some even shorter, and most were written by copy boys. We received five dollars for a story. They were straightforward pieces—"Love thy neighbor was the theme of the sermon yesterday at . . ." was a typical beginning. This is the way they had been written for years and it was the way the religion editor, a kindly gentleman named George Dugan, thought it should be done. He never made a change in your copy without smiling first.

If there was a type of story that typified the *Times*, it was the sermon: straight, no-frills, the way we've always done it. The *Times* was an editor's paper, as opposed to a writer's paper.

I was no rebel, but I did try to jazz up these little pieces, sometimes by interviewing the priest or minister after his talk and adding something else—perhaps even a different slant. It was a challenge to make things interesting. Soon, I was making myself known in churches all over town—in Harlem, at Adam Clayton Powell's Abyssinian Baptist Church, to Marble Collegiate on Fifth Avenue, where the nationally recognized author Norman Vincent Peale ("The Power of Positive Thinking") took the pulpit, to some storefront *iglesia* in Brooklyn. I would invariably take a seat in the front row, take out my notepad (tape recorders weren't practical; they were as large as a coffee-table book back then), and write while the minister was speaking.

In Harlem, I was feted after the services with lunch from the parishioners, who were proud that someone from the *New York Times* had come to their community. Soon, I started taking women I was dating to services. I guess it was a thrill for a college girl to go on a real live newspaper assignment. And then the next day, she'd see the story in the paper written by the guy she had gone out with.

After one sermon, the minister approached me and wondered why I was writing while he was speaking. I told him who I was and he said, "Why don't you just ask for a copy of my sermon?" And so, whenever I was going to church that Sunday, I called in advance, spoke to the minister, and got a copy of the sermon after services. Sometimes, they even mailed one to me in advance.

These Monday stories were terrific building blocks. Until then, the only stories any of us had written were for the college paper. I don't want to minimize the importance of writing for the school newspaper. But generally, they were not deadline pieces. Our paper at City College came out twice a week; now, in the *Times,* I was sitting down at about 2 P.M. and had to be done in a few hours. That was the key—it had to be finished. The dog couldn't eat your homework. Not only was writing it fairly quickly a necessity but also you had to make it interesting, and it had to be factually correct—the minister's name, the church, the street address. It may not seem like such a big deal, but it was a start.

I also realized that every section in the paper needed copy. The paper didn't write itself. Sports was especially hungry for stories in the Sunday paper. It was the only day of the week that Sports had a stand-alone section. For six days a week, the *Times* printed a two-section paper. Sports could be in either section, buried in the back or the middle. For Sunday's paper, the early edition had a copy deadline of 4:30 P.M. on Saturday, and while many college games were over by that time, there were many more that weren't. So we had to hold the space with stories that were killed for a live one in the later editions.

I scoured New York for these space-holding stories. But they required more talent than writing a sermon. They usually were "features" as opposed to news. No "love thy neighbor" leads. Instead, they had to be clever enough to hold the reader's attention, but not puerile. This was no exercise writing for a journalism class. This was the real thing. And I knew I would be judged on these pieces if I were to ever make reporter at the paper. It would be my body of work. Another thing: in the Sunday *Times,*

I would get a byline if the piece was long enough. You never got your name over a sermon.

So one night, walking on the boardwalk at Coney Island, I noticed that the pier in front of the famed parachute jump was filled with people. It turned out they were fishing—they did this every night, many coming with lanterns, others with books, some with families.

It made a story. I had a byline.

I saw a parrot on a man's shoulder outside a Brooklyn courthouse. Turns out the owner and his bird were hauled into court because the parrot cursed the neighbors. Another story, humorous at that. When I went to the racetrack one night, I gave my car to be valet-parked. After the last race, I handed my ticket to a valet—and was impressed by the rodeolike scene of cars and drivers darting to and fro. It made a story, although the Internal Revenue Service saw the piece, in which I wrote about the tips handed out, and questioned the drivers on their tax returns. After another foray to the track, I wondered about the bugler—the fellow who calls the horses to the races. He was a guy named Joe, he played the trumpet at the Philharmonic, and he was a story.

These were the kinds of pieces we eager young fellows watched out for—our driving force was to figure out how could we get into the paper. It was the way other writers such as David Halberstam and Gay Talese had started. I looked in a big, ledger-like book we called our "Advance Book"—it contained every sports event going on, locally and nationally, on a daily basis. If I saw something interesting that was easy enough to reach, I'd volunteer: high school soccer championships, stories on cheerleaders, cricket in Central Park—anything, just let me write, let me see my name in the paper. Once, driving in Upstate New York, I saw some people wearing Middle European costumes getting out of a car. They were headed toward the annual onion-harvest festival, an event their ancestors brought over from Poland. It wasn't much of a story, maybe two hundred words. But it got in the paper.

I believe that starting like this—as opposed to coming into the business out of journalism school, say—forged a passion for writing. It was a thrill to see my name in the paper, a thrill to see anything I wrote in the paper, even without a byline. I don't know whether this was a calling—well, yes, I think it was. It also helped create a bond among all of us who were copy boys. And once we had made it, we understood we had achieved something thanks to our shared passions.

A few years ahead of me on the paper were Halberstam, Talese, Bob Lipsyte, and Howard Tuckner. They all had been copy boys, too, and so for someone like me, seeing their names, seeing the quality of their stories, the nature of their assignments, gave me hope that perhaps I could be part of that strand. Talese, Lipsyte, and Tuckner all had been copy boys in sports as well.

The public probably has forgotten Howie Tuckner. He was one of the brightest young reporters on the paper. He was always willing to look over my copy before I anxiously turned it in. He encouraged me to throw in an adjective or two, to dispel my fears of being too forward in my writing.

Howie saw himself as the best writer in the sports department. But he wanted the football Giants' beat. It was one of the prestigious assignments. Instead, the paper asked him to cover the Jets. He quit, rather than to take what he viewed as second-best. He called me over one afternoon and said, "Well, kid, you've got an opening now. I'm leaving."

Howie went on to become a Vietnam correspondent for NBC, then ABC. In one infamous episode on camera, a shell exploded nearby and shrapnel made a hole in his pants near his crotch. He knew he couldn't get it on camera, so he directed the cameras to start rolling again—and re-created the injury, but avoided the crotch area. The last time I saw him, he was back in the States and doing a piece at the mayor's office in Gracie Mansion. He was complaining about the way his talent was not recognized. A few weeks later, he went to the roof of his mother's apartment house in the Bronx and jumped off.

I always admired Howie for his exceptional good looks and his understated way of talking. Even the way he had told me he was quitting the paper was said in a whisper. But he was right about one thing: his departure did create an opening.

Forty years later, I remember the day I became a reporter. The sports editor, Jim Roach, told me they liked my work, and were going to start me off at a salary that reporters weren't supposed to reach until their second year—$186 a week. I called my fiancée, Roz, at the school where she was teaching.

"All our troubles are over," she exclaimed.

10

Last Call for Brooklyn

Becoming a reporter, and getting married, occurred at virtually the same time and took me out of my beloved Brooklyn, but into the arms of my wife. Brooklyn was where I had grown up, learned about sports, loved and lost the Dodgers, played on the streets. I think about it still.

Everyone's home is a state of mind. I'm sure there are people from small towns who think back to their childhood and can't imagine a more perfect start. There are grown-ups whose parents were farmers, and the memory of 6 A.M. milkings must seem like perfection. But New Yorkers, and I'm not talking about Syracuse, have a different type of memory—it's not of trees or parks or alfalfa or the village square. For many of us, it is the games we played and the unique way we made the streets the focus of those games.

In ways I still don't understand, I'm sure these formed my reaction to the sports I covered. Perhaps my appreciation for the beau geste—such as the pirouette the clever defenseman for the Montreal Canadiens, J. C. Tremblay, employed—was a carry-over from watching someone on roller skates avoid hitting a bus. Or the way I enjoyed seeing Phil Rizzuto of the Yankees lay down a bunt and beating it out to first resonated because he used guile instead of strength, something I could relate to. And the teams I follow today are the overachievers, those with a history of problems that they somehow overcome. I'm not much interested in the Notre Dames or the Yankees or the Dallas Cowboys. They don't need me. They've got enough fans rooting them on.

I suppose people who write about themselves and their work think back to childhood, and how their family shaped them. My mother, Adella, an industrious woman ahead of her time—she used to attend socialist meetings, taught me about writers in the *New Yorker,* gave me bits and pieces of Hollywood lore—had no time for, nor interest in, sports. She had divorced my father when I was a year old and raised me on the second floor, which we shared with her mother, stepfather, and half brother. A tenant, who paid thirty-four dollars a month (my grandfather owned the two-story house), had the first floor.

My uncle Arthur, her half brother, was a fan. My earliest sports memory is listening with him to the 1946 baseball All-Star game, in which Ted Williams got four hits. From that moment on, Williams was this ten-year-old's idol. I grew even more enamored of him, found him a kindred soul, when I learned that his mother had raised him following a divorce, too. When I met him more than forty years later—at the Hall of Fame in Cooperstown, New York—I was concerned about how to start a conversation.

"You should have seen your face," said my son Mike. "You looked like a kid in awe of a hero." I was fifty-two years old, had written a dozen books, and had been a reporter for almost thirty years. Mike was right, though.

Arthur took me around when he played sandlot games. I went with him to Ebbets Field; he took me to football games. The newspapers in the house were the *Post* and the *Mirror.* My grandparents read the Yiddish-language "Forward." In my neighborhood, you read the *Times* when you were looking for a job, or your high school teacher told you to.

My father, Al, was a man I knew only on weekends—and even then, not consistently. His failing, besides his temper and his inability to take care of obligations such as my mother and me, was his gambling.

The other men in my life were my twin uncles—actually, my mother's stepbrothers. Their names were Solly and Hymie. Both were bookies, both constantly skirting the law—and yet almost Hollywood figures to me. They grew up in the Roaring Twenties, their pals were henchmen of the infamous Murder Incorporated crew, and when they weren't at home lived a life that George Raft glamorized in the movies.

I was emotionally closer to Solly, who lived only two blocks away. His oldest daughter, Renee, was brilliant, with no patience for stupidity. She was a year older than I, and I looked up to her—she taught me how to touch-type and rapped my knuckles if I looked at the keys. She was a math whiz, often helping her father figure out complicated betting pay-offs. She taught me how to decipher cryptogram word games and helped me get through arcane mathematical formulas.

Her mother, Jean, had been a dime-a-dance hostess back in the day, but she also was a savvy wisecracker. I loved being at their house. It had a mother and a father.

I must admit that Sol, except for Sunday mornings, wasn't usually around. For after his workday, he would spend the evening with a girl-friend at Jack Dempsey's restaurant in Times Square, or at Runyonesque all-night floating crap games—and sometimes even in jail overnight when the cops raided the games, or were under orders by the mayor's office to pick up bookmakers. When I joined the paper's sports depart-ment, a cheer went up in Sol's family—I could get free tickets to the racetrack. I could even get inside information, they thought.

I think about Sol (and Renee, who never used her brilliance once she left her teen years) as I wonder about my comfort with some of those people on the edge of the law I came across in later years. I understand why they grip me. Still, gambling was anathema to me. My maternal grandmother had always spoken angrily about my father's gambling. My grandmother's second husband, whom I called "grandpa" and loved as dearly as my grandmother, fascinated me with his propensity for card-playing with two other older men from the neighborhood. They had loud pinochle games, many hands ending with my grandfather throwing down his cards and shouting, in Yiddish, "I can't win and you can't lose!" They routinely barked at one another, calling the other "cheater" or worse, then would get back to the business of card-playing.

My grandfather always kept a drawer filled with loose change for his games. He knew exactly how much money was in that drawer. Every day he counted it.

My gambling low point came in 1951. I know it was 1951, because every sports fan of the day remembers that year, when my Dodgers had an insurmountable August lead over the Giants. The lead, in fact, once reached 13½ games. As that edge slowly eroded, now down to 10 games, the neighborhood tough guy, whose first name was Patsy, started making fun of the Dodgers. The Giants, he claimed, would catch them. Patsy was fourteen years old, my age. But he was a squat fireplug of a boy, so strong that he was able to lift a few inches off the ground a new, small car called the Henry J, built by a now-defunct carmaker, Kaiser-Frazer. No one messed with Patsy. I got tired of his bragging, though, and told him the Dodgers would win the pennant, easily.

"Wanna bet?" he asked. It was a dare, and I took it. "You gotta give me odds," he said. I gave him 3-to-1—my three dollars to his one the Dodgers would win.

Now let me concede right now: everyone from Brooklyn has a story about Bobby Thomson's home run—the "shot heard 'round the world." It gave the Giants the pennant over the Dodgers with a playoff victory. Everyone knows what they were doing at that moment, or says they do. I do.

I started to worry about that three dollars late in September, when the Giants inched closer, and then they tied the Dodgers, forcing a three-game playoff. It went to Game 3, which was played, of course, in the afternoon.

My French class at Thomas Jefferson High School ended at 3:50 P.M. Everyone dashed into the hallway and someone hauled out a portable radio. There was a roar as Bobby Thomson connected with a Ralph Branca pitch, and then the hysterical Russ Hodges, the Giants' broadcaster, kept screaming in what became a famous litany, "The Giants win the pennant, the Giants win the pennant, the Giants . . ."

The time was about 3:54, says memory. I walked home crestfallen not only for my loss of that moment, but for my impending loss of the three dollars, which I did not have nor could imagine any way I would.

That day, I stayed in the house after getting home. I did that for the next few days as well, afraid to go outside and come across the dreaded Patsy. We never made plans to meet friends back then. We simply knew we'd see one another sometime on the street.

On a Saturday morning, another friend came to my house about ten o'clock. I should have known he could not be trusted. He was fat, and he used to pour Pepsi-Cola over his Frosted Flakes cereal for breakfast. He turned out to be my Iago, for he lured me downstairs, saying he wanted to throw a ball around.

The moment I walked outside the door, Patsy appeared. "Where's my money?" he demanded. I didn't think he really expected to collect all of the three dollars. I told him I didn't have it.

He grabbed my right arm and twisted it behind me, inflicting the greatest pain I had ever felt. I screamed. Then I cried. I promised to get him the money and he let me go.

My mother gave me the money. She told me I shouldn't have bet, but said I had to honor it. I knew that three dollars meant a lot to her.

Patsy got his money, and I never made another bet on a baseball game. Over the years, my father did, though, losing considerably more than three dollars. Once, he even called me at the paper when I was a copy boy, and wanted to hatch a scheme in which I would get him the horse-racing results before his bookie did. Then, he figured, he could get a bet down on a horse that already had won.

Forty years later, I wrote a story about the anniversary of Thomson's shot against Branca. In a way, it was closure for me. I felt an intimate part of their shared moment, for that had been a significant event in my life, too. I called Branca. I called Thomson. I never called Patsy. Still, I chuckled when I wrote the story of that epic home run and the effect it had on people's lives. Here I was getting paid for it. I made back that three dollars, finally.

Why do I think of that home run still? I'm glad I do, because it tells me something about the power of sport, and I never want to lose that perspective. It also tells me something about growing up and the forces that shape you. I know they made me a better writer.

Funny, but over the years, when I've interviewed ballplayers of all stripes, I invariably ask about their family background. I'm fascinated with how other people grew up. Did they have Sunday dinners with their parents? Did their fathers take them to ball games? What impact on your athletic career did your father have? Your mother?

Do I ask these to get a better story? Yes. But I also ask, I'm sure, because I want to know what longings they may have had for the perfect family. I think I've finally realized that it's fruitless to search for that paradigm, or to expect one myself. You're happy within your own context.

Yet approaching forty years of marriage as I write this, with three children and four grandchildren, I believe I'm happy, very happy.

Did Tolstoy get it right when he said, "All happy families resemble one another, but each unhappy family is unhappy in its own way"? I'm not sure, after interviewing so many people. Tolstoy was facile. I never came across two people whose stories were identical.

These days, though, I don't interview players and say, "Tell me about your father and mother." So many of the athletes I write about didn't have a traditional upbringing. They are children of divorce—or maybe never had parents who were married. So I couch my question. "Tell me about growing up," I say, or ask, "Who influenced you as a child?" Then I hear about aunts and grandparents.

If someone were to ask about how my upbringing shaped my sportswriting, I'd also tell him or her that our games were unique to the sidewalks of New York. They were devised by children whose parents never paid two bits for a seat at the ballpark, or even knew what a park was—for the games involved the apartment house, the stoop of the small wooden houses, the rectangular-shaped boxes that made up the concrete sidewalks, the "sewers," the manhole covers.

Forget about ball fields and uniforms and Little League. There weren't any. At least, I never saw one in my corner of the world. Instead, from the time I was nine or ten, I remember playing every game—baseball, football, punchball, tag, hide-and-seek, stickball, kick-the-can, touch football, handball, box baseball, triangle—either in front of my house, on my street, or around the corner. So did all my friends. Maybe later, when we were thirteen or fourteen, we forayed into other, more dangerous neighborhoods, even as far as deserted dirt farms that we turned into our own fields of dreams.

The rubber sphere of choice, the ball, was that little pink ball we mispronounced as "spaldeen." It was a rubber ball that bounced, or could be squeezed, made by Spalding's. It was ubiquitous. You could play by yourself with a spaldeen, you could come up with a game for two, or three, or more. Most of us started out by simply playing in front of our houses, in some variation of baseball. Of course, this was not baseball as the rule books described it—rather a game that was geared to a few people, one ball, sometimes no bat.

These were games of exquisite precision, because they took place in confined areas. No white-chalked foul lines, no first-down markers, no basketball courts. When you played a game in someone's face, you learned to use guile, deceit, head-fakes, arm-fakes. You learned, in short, to be a New Yorker—or at least, what other people thought of as a New Yorker. For we worked in close quarters. Then again, our life was in close quarters. I lived on a street of two-story buildings. Each one either had families on both floors, or a store below, a family above. Sometimes, like the grocer's across the street, the family lived behind the store. Everything you needed was on my side of the street, or across the street: the grocer, the butcher, the "French" cleaner's, the shoe store, the barber shop, the clothing store, the bicycle store. Two blocks down there was a bakery, on the next corner was the pharmacy, and next to that was the appliance store. Doctors, dentists, accountants, insurance brokers—all had shingles outside their houses. Your neighbors knew if you had a runny nose. My barber, four houses down, often would stop me while I was on my way to school and drag me in and splash some Brilliantine on my head and comb and brush my hair.

"Now you look like a man," he said.

If I got up very early, say 6:30, and Joe Schlaff, the grocer across the street, wasn't opened, my grandmother would write an I.O.U. with our name on it, and send me to take a bottle of milk from the big wooden cartons in front of the store, and leave the note on top.

Every school was within walking distance—the public school, the junior high, the high school. Thousands of children walked every day to these schools, passing the same stores.

This was the milieu in which we played.

For box baseball, you needed only three squares of cement sidewalk, which would serve as the "fields"—yours, a middle neutral zone, and your opponent's. You held the ball with the thumb and first two fingers and squeezed the pliable spaldeen into the other guy's box—maybe eight feet away from you. Squeezing it allowed you to put "English" on it, make it curve left or right, even stop short—the infamous "stopper"—or speed up. If he could hit it back to you, he got a single if it came on one bounce, a double on two, and so on. If he missed hitting the ball, he was out. Two kids, one ball, you could play nine innings or all day.

Then there were the games played against buildings—balls slapped off the sides of the apartment house, which became impromptu handball courts. Or the game of stoop-ball in front of my house: you threw the ball at the steps, and tried to catch the rebound on as few bounces as possible. A ball that hit the edge of the steps often would carom back at such a high speed it was dubbed a "killer."

But for sheer exuberance and freedom of movement, we had the street games, played in what we used to call the "gutter," our misnomer for the middle of the street, with pauses for passing cars.

There are expressions still around that only New Yorkers know or use —"a three-sewer hitter," for example. To be more accurate, it was really a three-manhole hitter. You stood on a manhole in the middle of the street in a game of punchball. You tossed the ball into the air—and punched it. If it sailed over the opponent's head, or bounced, it was in play. You ran to first base, which often was the tire of a car parked to your right down the block. Second was another manhole cover, in the middle of the street, third was another car's tire, and home was where you started. Accuracy was critical. If the ball sailed onto the sidewalk, it was an automatic out.

We all had the ability to hit the ball over the next sewer in front of us. Two sewers were even better. Three sewers? You were a local legend, a three-sewer hitter.

The real sewers, the ones under the curb that had open gratings on them, were another sort of home base. This was the game of triangle, hitting a ball, running across the street to another sewer, running back without getting tagged. You could play this game at night, under the streetlights, because it was all about running, not seeing a ball.

All these games were played in front of neighbors, who were anxious when you hit a ball—after all, the windows of their houses, or their car windows, could be smashed, and often were. So if one grown-up complained—and they all knew our names, even if our families weren't friends—we'd simply move up the block.

In the summers, street ball in all its forms was a passion from morning till night. We'd take a break about 7 P.M. to wait for "the papers." Every night, the *Mirror* and the *Daily News* would arrive at the candy stores, each of which had a newsstand. The papers were two cents apiece.

Although the Major League baseball games had ended only a few hours earlier, the papers had the stories, and the back-page headlines and the photos under them dominated the conversation. Night ball? It was a curiosity. Most games were played in the daylight, and when it was warm, some of my neighbors would take their bridge chairs onto the sidewalk, open a folding table, put a pitcher of lemonade on it, and set up a portable radio to hear the games. The game we are talking about was baseball.

There were no "issues" in the sports pages back then—no discussions about Title IX, or whether a team threatened to leave town if it didn't get a new stadium, or what's wrong with the Olympic movement, or of high school seniors with lousy SAT scores or a police record going to college. What mattered most was baseball, in season from April through October. And when the season ended, there was the Hot-Stove League in the winter, and soon there was the Grapefruit League, spring training in Florida. In between, you had football, you had basketball, you had hockey. Once their shorter seasons ended, that was it. Not a peep out of any of them for months.

In my corner of Brooklyn, the team was the Dodgers, the most human collection of athletes man has ever put together. They were a team of failed gods, a Sisyphus-like troupe destined to strive, get near the top, and then fall back down again. To a working-class neighborhood of Jews, Italians, and blacks, they also were a melting pot, the best idea of America in microcosm. Above them all was Jackie Robinson. Where else but in Brooklyn, we reasoned, would the first black Major League baseball player perform?

The captain was Harold (Pee Wee) Reese, whose name had a vaguely Jewish sound, but whose boyish southern charm and low-keyed approach to Robinson's arrival had set the tone for baseball's integration. There was the strong, silent Gil Hodges at first base, a World War II hero (he killed "Japs" bare-handed, we were told), who had such a terrible World Series one year, followed by a slump the next, that a minister took to his Brooklyn pulpit one Sunday to ask everyone to include Hodges in their prayers. There was the hard-luck Pete Reiser, who enjoyed a spectacular rookie year, but then got into the habit of running head-first into walls, receiving a series of concussions. There was the brooding Carl Furillo, darkly Italian, known as "Skoonj," with the rifle arm and vaguely menacing unshaved face. Even the manager, an unexciting fellow named Walter Alston, had at least an empathetic side: he had one Major League at bat to his credit, and had struck out.

The catcher was Roy Campanella, Campy, whose mother was black, his father Italian, and who had a witty style. The center fielder was the Duke of Flatbush—Duke Snider, the most gifted young player the Dodgers ever developed, but who had a penchant for swinging at bad pitches. Of course, to my neighborhood people with old-country accents, his name came out "Schneider."

In 1947, with Robinson's arrival (Campy came a year later) the Dodgers' dynasty was born, along with a phrase that became part of the language: "Wait Till Next Year!" For the damned Yankees always stopped us in the World Series. They had defeated us in 1941, when the Dodgers' twenty-one-year absence from the World Series ended; then, when the Dodgers got pretty good, but not good enough, the Yankees halted them in 1947, 1949, 1952, 1953. Our Brooks, also known in vaguely biblical terms as the Flock, had a fatal flaw that not even prayer could conquer.

Yet, this band of ballplayers—which included a pitcher nicknamed "Oisk," because that's the way the first syllable of "Erskine" was pronounced in Brooklyn—was more than just symbolic of our universal striving. They lived among us. Almost all had homes, or rented apartments, in Brooklyn. They had neighbors over for barbecues on off-days. You could see them bowling at Freddie Fitzsimmons' alleys. They went to the Loews Flatbush movie theater. The players that didn't car-pool took the subway to Ebbets Field. You could sit in the subway for five cents and have a good shot at talking to Duke Snider on your way to the game. After games, players would stand around and sign autographs for us. They were not New Yorkers, but they seemed to understand us.

The Dodgers even had their own poet—Marianne Moore, known as the poet-laureate of Brooklyn and a Dodger fan. One of her poems was titled, "Hometown Piece for Messrs. Alston and Reese." Besides the poet, we also had our own ballpark philharmonia. A group of men dressed like hobos, sitting behind first base, was called the Dodgers' Sym-Phony, playing a mix of Dixieland and Spike Jones atonal offerings that would have made Hindemith wince. The organist was Gladys Gooding, subject of the trick question, "Who was the only person to play for the Knicks, Rangers, and Dodgers in the same year?"

This was the background that formed my understanding of, and my feeling toward, sports. The heart mattered, and so did a sense of humor. Chaos also was good. We could never—ever—root for the Yankees, those bankers in pinstripes. The Giants, the third New York team, weren't relevant to us in Brooklyn. They might as well have been in Cincinnati.

Probably a million other Brooklynites shared the experience. The baseball writers, and the columnists, were our historians. The way they wrote was the way I hoped I could one day—smarmy, informed. I had this complete sportswriting jargon, vernacular I could not use in my school papers. But most important—they actually got to talk to these players, got to spend spring training in Florida, which had names to rival Shangri-La: Vero Beach, St. Petersburg, Fort Lauderdale. The writers got to travel with the team, got to sit in the press box.

One magical day, I was invited to Ebbets Field. All the sports editors of the Brooklyn high school newspapers were there, and we were being treated to our own press conference with Duke Snider. We sat behind home plate about three hours before a game, and the Dodgers' public relations director introduced Snider. He appeared in his uniform with the number 4, the "Dodgers" emblazoned in blue across the front of his white flannel shirt. It was my first taste of the celebrity life.

We were told to ask questions, and I had mine. The problem I had was how to frame it. For at this moment, I was trying to think like a sportswriter, trying to be professional, trying to strike a common chord with this future Hall of Fame ballplayer, one of several on the team I had idolized. In other words, how was I to be cool, professional? So in my best sportswriter-speak, or how I imagined sportswriters spoke, I asked the Duke: "What's the longest smash you ever clouted?" Spoken, I thought, like a back-page headline.

He gave me a thoughtful answer, even pointing to the spot in center field where he had clouted his smash.

Now, fifty years later, I still recall that question. It was the first of many, it turns out. And what I had only dreamed about—actually interviewing these gods in gray flannel—actually came true. Of course, when I finally met my heroes again, I was a grown man, and how could I tell them I had imitated their swing, or got their autograph, or knew their hometown?

I had gotten Jackie Robinson's autograph two or three times when he was a player and I waited outside the ballpark. The next time I saw him was at least a dozen years later, and he was the president of a football team that was trying to make it in a new league, playing in smaller stadiums. His outfit played on Randalls Island, off the tip of Manhattan.

The team wasn't doing well financially. So after the game, I sought him out. When I saw him, my first reaction was to tell him how much I had enjoyed watching him play, even tell him how he had given me autographs a few times. I wanted to talk to him about his Dodger years and how I had followed the team—how I had given a speech about his life to the entire school in the auditorium when I was in the sixth grade at P.S. 158. Now, though, I had to put away childish things. I asked him a question about the team's finances.

He glowered. I've lost that connection between us forever, I thought.

I wrote my story, noting that he was a bit displeased at any suggestion the football team wouldn't make it.

The next day, my sports editor wrote me a note that began, "An angry Jackie Robinson called to say he was not angry, as your story said."

Over the years I progressed from covering sports in Randalls Island. One night I was on Bill Mazer's radio show at the Plaza Hotel, plugging a book I had written, when someone handed Bill a news item: Jackie Robinson had died. Mazer's producer made a hurried call, and one of the town's baseball writers showed up to be interviewed. Bill apologized to me, but he said he had to do the rest of the show about Jackie Robinson.

I thought, "Then you should be talking to me." I never got a chance to give Jackie a send-off. I was replaced on the air by the baseball writer.

I did get a chance to meet some of those other Dodgers whom Roger Kahn (with a nod to Dylan Thomas) had elegantly described as "the Boys of Summer." But although our conversations were much more cordial than the one I had with Jackie, I always left feeling I had not said what really had been on my mind.

Then again, how do you thank someone for part of your childhood?

11

Northern Exposure

Ah, to be a baseball writer now that spring is here. The baseball writer was the elite of the profession. I was to learn they looked with disdain at most of the other sports beats. And yet, barely a year after I became a reporter, I was asked to cover a hockey game. I was open-minded about writing hockey. But a hockey game to a baseball writer is a Park Avenue matron's idea of a third-floor walk-up. Vic Ziegel, my City College classmate and future baseball writer and columnist for the *Post* and *News*, described hockey with disdain as "soccer on the rocks."

I had never seen a hockey game until I wrote about one. This was how much importance the *Times* attached to hockey back then: It was October 1964, and I came into the office around noon. I was the "office reporter"—manning the phones, ready to write a breaking story, or to handle an obituary. It was a mandatory part of the sports department. A reporter had to be in the office every day.

About 2 P.M., the assistant sports editor, Jim Tuite, realized the Rangers were opening their season that night, in Boston, and we had not assigned anyone to cover the game. That was the benign neglect with which we treated hockey. We didn't always send someone on the road with the Rangers, who had only five opponents then—Boston, Chicago, Detroit, Montreal, and Toronto. We didn't even cover the Stanley Cup championships if it wasn't convenient for us.

I was able to catch a six o'clock flight to Boston, and got to the old,

143

noisy Boston Garden while the National Anthem was being played. Luckily, I had bought a *World-Telegram* at the airport and read an advance story on the season's opener. I at least had a fan's knowledge of what this was all about as I prepared to cover my first event outside of New York.

I had barely opened up my typewriter case when the whoosh of the game started with the dropping of the puck, and then everyone started flying around the ice, while around me people were screaming and cursing and I felt the press box shaking dangerously. I had never seen such action, heard such noise (the old building's cramped quarters magnified sound to such an extent, you could hear the blades crackling on the ice).

Well, I think the final score was 9–5, an extraordinary number of goals for that era, when the average hockey score was 3–2. I had seen my first hockey fight as well, instigated by a Bruin named Reggie Fleming, whom I promptly dubbed Reggie the Ruffian. I used the word "incredible" in my lead, and how the conservative paper allowed me to get away with it, I'll never know. But I wrote about the fighting and the passion and the noise. I was ecstatic.

After the game was over, I had no place to sleep. I had forgotten to book a hotel room. But the Rangers didn't have a hotel, either. And they didn't charter airplanes back then. Instead, to save money, they stayed overnight in the rail yards in Boston in a sleeper car. In the morning, the engine was attached to the cars. For the same buck, the Rangers got transportation back to New York as well as a place to sleep.

The club's public relations director, a whimsical fellow named John Halligan, invited me to spend the night in a Pullman. I got there before midnight, and went to bed. About 2 AM. I woke up. The car was being attached to an engine for the trip back to New York. We pulled into Grand Central Station at about 7 in the morning.

At noon, after going home to shower and have breakfast, I went back to the office and Tuite told me there was a lot of buzz about my story. I understood why. Hockey had rarely been covered by younger writers, or even the top ones on most papers. The joke in New York was that there were 15,925 hockey fans, and that they all were at the Rangers game at Madison Square Garden. The papers didn't have to expend time and space on hockey for its narrow audience.

I was in my late twenties, and yet was the second-youngest reporter in sports. The fellow who had been our occasional hockey writer was a jack-of-all-trades who was as likely to cover an amateur soccer game as the Rangers. He also was an old-school writer, given to leads such as, "The New York Rangers scored twice in the third period last night to defeat the Toronto Maple Leafs before 15,925 fans at Madison Square Garden." Straightforward, all the facts, the who, the what, the when, the how, just as generations of *New York Times* sportswriters had done, had been taught to do.

Luckily, I was so enthralled with my first game that I had been able to capture the excitement in my story. The next day, I was asked to cover a Rangers' workout.

That began an eight-year stretch as the paper's hockey writer. It took me to Canada, where I learned to appreciate the hold one sport can have on a country. Indeed, hockey to Canadians is part of their life to an extent greater than baseball is to those of us in the United States. But how could I make Americans (a term some Canadians object to if it's used to describe people in the States; Canadians, after all, are North Americans) aware of this? And how could I get New York sports fans to care?

It wasn't that I saw myself as an ambassador of the sport, but if I was going to cover that sport, I wanted to imbue it with an importance. Sure, my ego was in the way. But I also believed it had an excitement and a history that could capture my readers.

Every player in the NHL back then was Canadian. Six teams, 120 players, 120 Canadians. Once in a while, an American-born player would pop up, then go back to the minors. Every few years, someone born in Sweden might make an appearance. It was, however, the Canadian thing.

The players were different from the athletes I had come to know in the States. Few Canadians were theatrical, or hot-doggers. They often were self-effacing, low-keyed. I soon understood why. The Canadian system of hockey was insidious. It took the gifted young players, who were identified when they were ten or eleven years old, and then sent them away from home to play junior hockey. They had learned from their first teams that winning came first, that they played with broken teeth—it carried over into their big-league careers. Little League mothers in the United States never would have put up with this attitude. But at fourteen, the gifted players signed "C" cards, or letters of intent, that effectively bound the player to a team for his career.

To play junior hockey often meant traveling hundreds of miles, moving away from friends and family, if a youngster's hometown did not have a top-quality team. There, in a new city far from home, the junior hockey player usually roomed with a family or was sent to a boarding school. He would play sixty games a year, often getting up at five o'clock in the morning for practice. He also was expected to attend school. Small wonder that when I started covering hockey in the 1960s, three-quarters of the NHL players never even were graduated from high school.

I wrote about this, and other aspects of hockey players' lives. I often traveled on their train rides (the vehicle of choice for many clubs back then). Once, I spent an evening in his private car with David Molson, the beer family heir who was the president of the Montreal Canadiens, talking politics and hockey and relations between the two countries.

I learned that hockey fans in the States had little knowledge of the behind-the-scenes aspect of the game, its politics, its hold on another country. Along the way, I wrote five books in five years. Every time I had a hockey idea, a publisher wanted it.

Perhaps twenty to thirty times a year, I would be the between-period guest on radio or television broadcasts of the games—both for the home team and the visitors. When you figure that every game was broadcast by both the home and away radio stations, and often by a television station as well, and there were two intermissions—well, TV and radio needed a lot of between-periods guests. Usually, these little spots were accompanied by gift certificates from the sponsors. There would be meals from restaurants, or sporting goods, or clothing, or simply twenty-five-dollar checks. I collected so many of these that I was able to barter some with another hockey writer who was in demand, Mark Mulvoy of *Sports Illustrated,* who went on to become its editor-in-chief for many years.

There was one gift I wish I hadn't taken.

I had gone on Rangers' radio broadcasts with my friend Marv Albert many times. He had not yet become a noted national personality, but in New York he was the voice of the Knicks and Rangers. He had his deep voice, knowledge of the game, which he painted extremely well, and his signature exclamations: "Kick save—and a beauty!" for the Rangers, and a resounding "Yes!" for a Knicks' basket. One of Marv's sponsors was a Midtown Manhattan restaurant named Chandler's, since defunct. As payment for going on with him, Marv gave me a gift certificate for two for dinner at Chandler's.

My wife and I decided to make an evening of it. We did not realize what a night it would be. Our plan was dinner, followed by a Woody Allen movie. We finished dinner, the check came, and I handed the waiter the gift certificate. He looked at it and asked me, "What's this?" The first pangs arrived with that question.

He brought the maitre d' over. He also looked at the piece of paper, then said, "Oh, we didn't do too well with this promotion, so we canceled it."

"Fine," I replied, "but before you did, you invited me for dinner."

He left to make a call, and came back and said, "We won't honor it."

In life, you don't get many chances to take a stand, even over issues such as a freebie (or not) dinner. I decided that this was my moment.

"Well, I won't pay it," I said.

"I'll call the police," he said.

I told him to go ahead, figuring it was a bluff. He asked us to wait near the front door. Within minutes two policemen showed up. The maitre d' told him I was "a wise guy," and trying to get something for nothing; I showed the cop the invitation.

"Just a minute," replied the officer. He called the station house. He got off the phone and told me I had to pay. I told him no. He said he would have to arrest me if someone signed a complaint.

From out of nowhere, the restaurant owner, who had actually signed my invitation, showed up to sign again—this time, putting his signature on the complaint. I was under arrest.

Well, the cops were very nice about it. "Should we cuff him?" asked the younger one. "Nah, he's OK," said the older one, as they put me in their patrol car. Roz, of course, could not come along for the ride. She was given instructions on how to get to the station house.

Sports commentator Marv Albert. Photo courtesy of TNT Sports.

There, the desk sergeant was asked which cell I should go in. He looked at the complaint and said I could sit down near him while the paperwork was being processed. Just then, my wife walked in. Prisoners in holding cells, most of them prostitutes, could see her. She had a cold sore on her lips, which had turned into a welt.

"What's the matter, honey? Did he beat you?" One of the prostitutes asked, solicitously.

I got fingerprinted (the officer gave his gun to someone to hold; he explained to me that another cop had once been shot by the "perp" during fingerprinting). Then the nice policeman said he was going to take my picture. I had to hold a board with a number under my face—you know, the mug shot. The problem was, the policeman didn't know how to use the Polaroid camera. My wife explained it to him, and he took the photo.

"You want another one for yourself?" he asked.

Then I had to pass the test to be released without bail. They asked: Did I have a job? Was I married? Did I live in the same place more than a year? Did I visit my mother? Each answer was worth points. I garnered enough points to get released.

Two days later, my lawyer sued Chandler's for $750,000 for false arrest. I was in my office when my phone rang. It was Marv.

Marv Albert has a forceful persona on radio and television. But I always thought of him as kind of shy. Once, at a New Year's party at my house, he seemed embarrassed when someone told a slightly off-color joke. At the time of the Chandler's incident, Marv was by no means a national celebrity—and thirty years from being a notorious one, at that. That happened when a spurned lover charged him with forcible sodomy. She also claimed he bit her on the back. He pleaded guilty to a misdemeanor assault charge, served no jail time, and his conviction eventually was wiped from his record.

But that was in the future. I picked up the phone to speak to Marv.

"Jerry, this is Marv Albert," he said. "Jerry—you've got to behave yourself!"

I tried to soothe Marv's fears that his reputation had been besmirched. I explained that I had legitimately tried to get the restaurant to honor the free dinner. We said good-bye, with Marv sounding a bit relieved.

A few minutes later, my lawyer called. Chandler's wanted to settle for $7,500 and avoid a costly false-arrest suit. "Take it," my lawyer counseled. "All it cost you was some embarrassment."

I took it, and promised my wife a mink coat to compensate for her run-in with the ladies of the evening. But the kids were growing, the bills were coming in, and she never asked for the mink. Come to think of it, I owe her one.

12

Stories that Readers Only
Knew the Half Of

"Ass-fuck?" I repeated. "Is that what you said?"

"Yes, ass-fuck," my editor replied. "That's how the name of Jim McMahon's acupuncturist translates into English."

My assignment: check that story.

This was back in 1986, Super Bowl week. McMahon, the Chicago Bears' quirky quarterback, had already mooned a photographer, who was trying to take pictures from a low-flying airplane during practice. Now, McMahon was claiming his acupuncturist's name was . . . well, it already was in the *New York Times*, but it wasn't going in again.

I had written a piece about McMahon and his Chinese acupuncture guru. Someone on our foreign desk called to say that . . . oops!—we'd been had, that the man's name translates to "ass-fuck." I was asked to verify this. So I dutifully called the Bears' public relations director—as if he had nothing else to do two days before the Super Bowl—and told him what the foreign desk guy said. The Bears' man adamantly denied it, claiming, "I got the spelling from the acupuncturist himself."

And perhaps he really did. On the other hand, maybe something was lost (added?) in translation. This acupuncturist, however, was an ongoing story, and I wanted to use his name again the following day. I was vetoed. No more using the nice man's name, whatever it was.

But I got in a few other words over the years, in more than eight thousand stories. Most of them were under deadline pressure. At the moment I crafted them—some, I admit, were hastily generated—I didn't always realize they were important or had legs—could stand up, could make a difference, meant something beyond filling a space of seven hundred or eight hundred words.

Yet certain of those stories transformed me. And perhaps, once in a while, I helped transform the reader, or the business, or maybe even some small part of American life. Along the way, there were stories like the one above, that had to be slightly fudged, or which I had information that I could not share fully at the time, or which, knowing my paper's rules on taste, I kept to myself.

There was one involving Joe DiMaggio, for example. I was doing a piece about the memorabilia craze of the early nineties—Pete Rose's bats, an autographed DiMaggio ball, a signed letter from Babe Ruth. The collector everyone pointed me to was named Barry Halper. The word "collector" wasn't big enough to describe the breadth of his activities. He had raised memorabilia to part science, part art. Barry also was a 1 percent owner of the Yankees, which put him in a good place to collect items that one day would be worth considerably more than he was paying for them.

I rang the bell to his New Jersey home. It played "Take me out to the ball game."

He took me down to his basement, past cases and drawers teeming with caps and balls and letters. There in the middle of the floor was a larger-than-life wax statue of the rotund, porcine-faced Babe Ruth—acquired from Madame Tussaud's museum in London. This was just a start.

Behind a door, Barry had one of those revolving clothing machines you see in dry-cleaning stores—press a number, and the garment appears on a pulley. Well, on his contraption he had a uniform worn by virtually every member of the Baseball Hall of Fame. He was missing only two.

He had a unique approach to important correspondence. He acquired one letter signed by Babe Ruth, for example, and then had Willie Mays and Hank Aaron sign at the bottom—giving him in one letter the autographs of the top three home-run hitters at that time in baseball history. He had bats and balls, the legendary Honus Wagner tobacco-company baseball card (taken out of circulation because Wagner did not smoke), and original signed contracts of some of the greats.

Along the way in his passion for the game, Barry also became very friendly with DiMaggio. At major events in DiMaggio's life, a birthday or a "day" at a ballpark, Barry was there. DiMaggio chose his friends very carefully. He was always worried about his privacy, people prying, and he obsessively avoided any mention of his marriage to Marilyn Monroe.

"One night," Barry related, "we were driving home after his sixty-fifth birthday party, and Joe started to talk about Marilyn. He didn't often do that. Soon he fell asleep, and I guess it was sort of a half-sleep. I hit a bump in the road and Joe woke up and blurted out, 'The sons-of-bitches killed her.' Then he went back to sleep. I guess he was talking about the Kennedys."

It was an extraordinary insight into DiMaggio's thinking—but it was told to me in confidence. I'm sure Barry didn't want the story repeated while Joe was alive. And another problem with it—the words "sons-of-bitches," in a way so eloquent, never would have found their way into the *Times*. The *Times* agonized for half a day back in 1961 whether to quote John F. Kennedy, who called the owners of steel companies "bastards."

Then there was my night with Brigitte—you know, Brigitte Nielsen, the spike-haired blonde who had been married to Sylvester Stallone.

The idea of the piece was a sort of at-home profile of the Jets' star defensive player, Mark Gastineau, and his inamorata, Nielsen. Mark was the best quarterback-chaser in pro football, and had become noted as well for his celebratory "sack dance," in which he pirouetted and whooped and hollered after sacking the quarterback. Now, he and Brigitte had found each other. The way I heard it was that the 6-foot 2-inch actress had seen his photo in the paper (Mark loved shaving his chest and having someone take a picture of his torso). Her people called his people, and the rest was history.

Our evening started out in a restaurant on the North Shore of Long Island, not far from where they had rented a home.

"People won't believe this, but I'm down on all fours cleaning the house," she told me. Well, sure, I could picture that.

She was a great storyteller, of how she had left home at sixteen and

The "New York Sack Exchange," in front of the New York Stock Exchange, 1981. Left to right: Joe Klecko, Marty Lyons, Abdul Salaam, Mark Gastineau. Courtesy of the New York Stock Exchange.

went to Rome to become a fashion model. Of how she was kidnapped for thirty-six hours during an uprising in the Seychelles, how she was almost trampled by adoring crowds in Rome, where they tend to live life like a Fellini movie. She never quite got around to telling us whether it was true, as legend has it, that she met Stallone by sending him a nude photo of her.

Brigitte and Mark invited us back to their house. Mark opened the front door, and said, "Well, what do you think?"

The house mirrored their personalities. On a wall overseeing the front room were two huge portraits—one of Nielsen's face, the other of the 6-foot-5 Mark's bare torso.

She led us into their bedroom. The huge pine bed was so high off the floor, there was a small ladder at its foot. Brigitte didn't need it. She dived onto the bed, started to roll around, and proclaimed, "This is where Mark and I spend all our time!"

Fine. But what could I do with it, print-wise? There was a wealth of interview material from the restaurant. But this particular moment? Again—*Times* sensibilities, or just good taste? I'm not sure, but on re-flection I should have tried to get that into the paper. It was more than X-rated talk; it was sort of fun. I guarantee you that if I had written that today (this happened in 1988), it would get into the paper.

Some stories didn't find their way into print because they had only personal meaning—yet told something about the people I was writing about. Such an event was my evening at Richard's.

Richard Todd was the Jets' quarterback who followed Joe Namath. Richard was a good guy who married a girl named Lulu. He invited me one offseason to visit him in Mobile, Alabama. I checked into a nearby hotel and set off to see him and his family for dinner. This was a few years before he got married.

I didn't know what to bring, so I stopped off to get some wine. When I went inside the store, I noticed it also was a pharmacy and a five-and-ten. In Alabama, you could buy wine in that kind of place. The wines were in a glassed-in refrigerator. I had never heard of any of the wines the store carried, so I picked out something that, if memory serves, was called "White French Wine," or maybe it was "French White Wine."

When I got to his house, Richard answered the door. I walked in and handed him the bottle of wine and he immediately called out with excitement, "Daddy—Jerry brought us some wine!" Well, everyone made a fuss over it. There was his mom (a professor of nursing), his dad (a professor of education at the University of South Alabama, or USA), his brother and sister-in-law, and his maiden aunt, Miz Duckworth.

The buffet spread was out of a party scene in *Gone With the Wind*: macaroni and cheese and collard greens and fried chicken and black-eyed peas and some other down-home dishes.

Then Dad—Carl Todd—had to open the wine.

"Uh, Richard, do you know where the corkscrew is?" asked Mr. Todd. They started going through the drawers. Carl Todd wasn't going to start the meal without opening the wine his guest had brought. But no corkscrew.

Richard then found a metal nail and began to pound it into the cork. Then he put a screwdriver to it and tried valiantly to get the cork up, or down, while all I could think of was the headline, "Jets' Quarterback Tears Open Thumb on Wine Brought by Reporter."

After a few minutes of screwing around, Richard couldn't get the cork to budge.

"C'mon, Jerry," said Richard cheerfully. "We'll go out and buy a corkscrew." So we left everyone at the dinner table and hopped into Richard's van. He put on his International Harvester cap at a jaunty angle and we went downtown. No corkscrew after repeated stops.

We went back to his house, where I suggested that maybe we could just push the cork in and strain the wine out. This sat well with father and son. Richard got himself a hammer and banged on the nail in the cork until he knocked it in.

Finally, Carl Todd poured the wine, which came out with bits of cork floating.

"Jerry," pronounced the elder Todd after a sip, "I 'spect this is the best bottle of wine I ever had."

How wonderfully gracious he was. Later I was to appreciate him even more when I found out he was a devout Baptist—who had never had wine before.

I think this is a great story, telling much about some people, and yet it didn't fit in a daily sports story. I was concerned whether it would have embarrassed Todd, whom I dealt with on a daily basis as the Jets' quarter-back. Eventually, though, I did write it for *Wine Spectator.* I'm not sure I wanted Richard to see the piece. I didn't want him coming off naively. I don't think he does.

I stayed with the Jets longer than I thought a newspaper reporter should. Early on I had figured that a "beat" writer would get to be too close to the people he wrote about, and that every four or five years it is best to move on. I always was concerned about, and remembered Lipp-mann's warning on, cronyism. But the Jets turned out to be beguiling. They practiced only fifteen minutes from where I lived. They played only once a week. They went on the road only eight games a year. They were, in short, a sportswriter's dream assignment—if that sportswriter relished having a home life.

Let's face it—there were moments of discomfort when I had to write about Namath or Todd having a bad game. After all, I'd be seeing them that same morning the paper came out. But maybe I was lucky, maybe they appreciated my honesty, maybe they thought I was attempting to be even-handed. Or maybe they just didn't want to make waves with the Gentleman from the *Times* (I dismiss this last possibility). I think that every athlete relates to honesty, even when it paints the player in some-thing less than a star's spotlight.

I sincerely believe, however, that athletes respect (or don't) the publi-cation or organization you are working for. And I had a built-in respect factor in working for my paper—which was largely unread, I'm sure, by most of the guys I wrote about. But it did have a reputation for fairness. I never was so naive as to believe that it was only me. I always was at-tached to the paper of record. It was my second name.

Speaking of naïveté, I was suckered by an angry caller named Harry Edwards back in 1965. I was the office reporter, and waiting for some-thing to break that I could expand on, to show the higher-ups what I could do. Out of the blue, Edwards phoned to complain about racism on Syracuse University's track team. He detailed a laundry-list of abuses and racial slurs directed by the coach toward black athletes, as well as to one of the Jewish runners.

These types of stories are minefields for the reporter. Too bad we don't get lessons in perspective. The easy thing for a writer to do when someone cries racism, or sexism, or uses any of the increasing number of adjectives that describe hatred directed at various groups is simply to report the charge. Then you get a comment—usually a denial—and run with it. Of course, the charge outweighs the denial.

I would say that back in '65, many of the journalistic techniques that the *Times,* and other papers, notably the *Washington Post* and *Boston Globe,* eventually adopted to ensure at least an attempt at fair reporting were not in place. One of them was independent corroboration, or at least a second source. Wasn't that a key tenet that Ben Bradlee, the *Post's* editor-in-chief, had insisted upon in the Watergate stories of Woodward and Bernstein almost ten years later? And since then, many stories simply have been spiked—never saw the light of day—because a reporter independently determined it did not have "legs," or was in a haze of unprovable half-truths.

This one wasn't, though. Edwards's story was so dynamic and dramatic—how this coach did not want blacks or Jews to compete, and how he made them miserable—that I got caught up in what I thought was a major story.

I should have gotten the coach's comment. As I recall, I did call but could not reach him. We should have held the story until I had. But it was a typical knee-jerk journalism reaction that continues unfortunately in journalism to this day. We had a story we were afraid would leak out, and so let's write it now before someone else gets wind of it.

Years later, I read about Patty Hearst's cross-country odyssey in her escape from California, when she was wanted for aiding the Symbionese Liberation Army in a bank robbery. The driver of that car? One of the Syracuse runners who allegedly had been discriminated against.

I have thought often of that incident and how irresponsible we can be in our business—how we simply don't always take the time to corroborate a story because some editor is hovering over us as deadline nears, and he wants that story. But I also believe that if the culture of a newspaper can be learned, or imparted, that you do the right, responsible thing, such blips can be minimized.

In fact, in the fall of 2002, ruminating about ways I could maximize my semi-retirement, I came up with an idea that seemed at once altruistic and enjoyable: hold seminars for new *Times* reporters. I know quite a bit about the paper—its history, its great stories, how it operates, where things are stored. Why, even back in college I had written a term paper on the history of the *Times*. I could also tell the young reporters about the nitty-gritty items such as where to go for information in this great big city, on subways or at City Hall or Shea Stadium. I would explain expense accounts and car rentals, too. I would warn about receiving gifts. I would talk about waiting until all the facts were in before getting caught up in the frenzy of a controversial story. I know about the paper's sense of self and the value it places on integrity. I would be one person who could make this plain to someone who was a neophyte New Yorker.

So I sent an e-mail to one of the assistant managing editors suggesting I do exactly that—breathe some life into the paper's tradition for newcomers. The letter was passed on to a key colleague, who thought it had merit and promised to look into it.

Some months later, the Jayson Blair scandal broke, an event that the publisher Arthur Sulzberger Jr. admitted was "a low point" in the paper's great history. Blair had fabricated quotes, had rewritten other newspapers' stories, had claimed to have visited places while never leaving New York. His dismissal was soon followed by the resignation of the paper's top two ranking editors—Howell Raines and Gerald Boyd.

I was saddened and bemused by the effect this scandal had in the newspaper business, as well as on my own paper. Not for a moment did I think I would have made a difference if I had been giving a seminar that Blair attended. Rather, I thought—still do—that anyone who would be willing to listen to me might have appreciated a bit more what it takes to be a responsible writer.

I think this sense of balance—of taking a step back, along with a deep breath—has helped me immeasurably. I recall being in an angry Jets locker room listening to their hotheaded linebacker, Bryan Cox, complain about being fined by the NFL for a pair of illegal hits to opposing players. The league's man in charge of meting out such punishment, Gene Washington, was black, too.

Cox branded him "a house Negro" and "token." Immediately, my colleagues started to write that down. Then Cox turned to me—I guess because I was older than the other writers, and had established a rapport with him as well—and said, "Don't you think there's racism here? What would you think it is if it's not racism?"

Bryan was in his element, of course. He was surrounded by mostly black teammates. He was a team leader and he was respected, perhaps even feared for his temperamental outbursts. Did he expect me to debate him right there? There was another thing about Cox and his outbursts. He did this all the time. He was the most heavily fined player in the history of the NFL, and he already had launched two lawsuits against the league. Clearly, this was a man who harbored some anger.

I told him this hardly was the place to bring up the issue. He understood that, and nodded. But I was faced with a dilemma. I knew all my colleagues would be writing this. I also knew that Cox deserved the fine. And why should he get a free shot at calling someone a "house Negro" simply because he's angry at getting caught on tape for breaking the rules? But cries of racism are generally heard, especially in sports, and especially when reporters are around to hear the charges.

I called my office, spoke my piece—I thought it was worth a "box" and not much more, and that we should tone down the rhetoric. I was overruled. I wrote nine hundred words about Cox and his claims, although I was able to point out his history of run-ins with authority.

Unlike in my earlier piece on Edwards's claims, I was able to reach someone for comment on Cox's negative charges. It was an NFL spokesman who said, simply, the league would not comment. By then, a policy had been established at our paper that you cannot simply quote someone who says something negative about another person without giving that person the opportunity to respond. That is, at the very least, fair play.

Another policy is directed at the "blind" negative quote (although no one seemed to worry about this in the Jayson Blair affair). It's the easiest thing in the world for someone to blast his boss, say, and hide anonymously. Of course, in matters of national importance, or corporate malfeasance, this is understandable. But in the less significant world of sports, it is a cheap and easy way to get back at someone without having to show your face. Thus, the *Times* tells its writers it rarely, if ever, will quote negative comments by anonymous sources. Of course, there have been exceptions, but generally these have been comments against big targets—the head of the U.S. Olympic Committee, or someone of that influence and power.

Another no-no at the *Times* now, and with which I agree: we don't tell the reader someone is threatening to sue. Anyone can threaten to sue. If they do, fine. But we shouldn't be using our pages for a trial balloon, to scare someone into submission.

I point out the Cox story because none of us gets it right all the time. Writing stories for newspapers presents a challenge each day. If you can handle the challenge with an overall philosophy, you may have been able to write something worthwhile. But one size doesn't fit all. Thus, some of us get overly excited when a hothead like Cox levels charges in anger. I'll bet he wouldn't have said the same things a day later.

It's always a tricky business to allow someone's anger to get in the way of a story, or to become a story. Yet we make value judgments about how and when to let that anger surface. Following is one instance where I actually was in the middle of a major confrontation. It indicates the difficulties and decisions we make in trying to balance good journalism with good sense.

It was in Montreal in 1972. It was the morning after the Soviet Union hockey team had bashed Team Canada in the opener of an epic series between the countries that was as much a Cold War battle as one for bragging rights on the ice. With that opening loss, Canada was questioning itself and its values because it had lost a hockey game to a bunch of foreigners.

So what did I have to do with it? Granted, I had a better seat than most in my role as a reporter. I also was collaborating on the autobiography of the Boston Bruins' big scorer, Phil Esposito, and this series, in which he was to star, would be the exclamation point to the book. But I also happened to be sitting in the middle of a remarkable confrontation on a train ride to Toronto between two key Canadian figures.

As an American, I fairly quickly grasped the importance of hockey to Canada. I used to love heading up to Kitchener, Ontario, every fall for the start of Rangers' training camp. There, I'd sit in the dimly lit arena, which was shaped like a cock-fighting amphitheater, and watch players' dreams unfold. The old men and young boys from town would watch, wearing their hockey jackets that proclaimed them "Tigers" or "Lions." I

immersed myself in the culture of hockey—observing the beery camaraderie after work, the cliché-driven motivations to excel, the total importance the sport had to these players and their families.

Why, even the Canadians' coach, Harry Sinden, understood what this
series against the Soviets would mean.

"Canada," he announced to his team during one locker-room seminar, "is first in the world in hockey and wheat. In that order." The
Canadian players had their first glimpse of the Soviets at a practice
session, and promptly made fun of their sticks and skates and old-
fashioned goalie masks.

My, my. Was Canada in for a shock.

Oh, the Canadians looked as if they would run away with the first
game. Before a few minutes elapsed, they led the Russians 2-0. But the
Soviets had this strange, non-Canadian way of looking at hockey, probably at all sports. They didn't get emotional. They weren't down emotionally, even though they were down on the scoreboard.

Soon, they sent goalie Ken Dryden sprawling in the Canadians' net by
capping off the most exquisite passing sequence I had ever seen. The
visitors went on to swamp the befuddled Dryden and the Canadians
7-3 in the opening game. It led the dour scoring star Frank Mahovlich
to say of the Soviets, "If you gave them a football, they'd win the Super
Bowl in two years." Canada was beating itself up.

I brought a bunch of newspapers the next morning when I boarded
the Turbo Train taking me to Game 2 in Toronto. In French and in
English, the headlines said it all:

"We Lost"

"Une **Leçon**"

"Le Canada **Ecrasé**"

The man who was the impetus for the games was Alan Eagleson, who
also was head of the Players Association. I knew him quite well. We
found each other on the train and sat together.

We barely had started to talk when all of a sudden, Ken Dryden's father loomed in the aisle. His goalie son had been whipped, castigated,
embarrassed. Now, Murray Dryden was a father instead of being a church
elder, Sunday school teacher, avuncular patron of kids' hockey.

"You suckered us!" shouted the goalie's old man. "What kind of scouting did you have? You told us we'd kill them. You made us think the Russians were a bunch of fools."

Eagleson jumped out of his seat and climbed over me. The pair started to argue, face-to-face. Dryden accused Eagleson of not doing enough groundwork to find out about the Soviets; Eagleson called Dryden a sore loser. Here were two cool customers, usually. They were at each other, though, for imagined misdeeds. Both were embarrassed by Canada's loss, yet neither had taken a slap shot, even put on skates.

The angst of Canada was being played out in front of me—really, a shock to the country's nervous system. Yet I never wrote this story. Should I have? This was not an event played out in front of paying customers. These were not competitors, albeit key figures. This wasn't even at a news conference, in front of the media. It happened to take place away from everyone except me.

My thinking on my decision was this: Yes, it would be a heck of a story, a sexy story, a story with Canada-wide implications. But I also thought the readers would be better served if I could keep both lines of communication open for future stories. In other words, Eagleson was someone I wrote about on a recurring basis. What good would it have done me to write this piece if I might have lost access in the future? After all, there was something confidential about this confrontation, or at least an implied confidentiality.

Come to think of it, the more I rationalize what I did, the more I wonder whether I shouldn't have written it. It really was a terrific story. If this had been in the States, and the subject had been baseball, I know I would have written the piece—imagine Yankee shortstop Derek Jeter's father fighting with Manager Joe Torre. Well, better late than never.

There have been times I even became part of the story, which is always a slippery slope for a writer. One particular piece was quite unusual, even dangerous, and my children always loved hearing me tell it.

My friends were curious one morning in the late 1970s when they picked up the paper, turned to international news, and saw my byline over a story about the death of an American Mafioso in Grenada. This is the Caribbean island (pronounced Gruh-nay-duh) that U.S. troops subsequently "invaded," for reasons having nothing to do with my story.

My story began one day when the sports editor received a phone call from a friend in the horse-racing business. The tale unfolded of a jockey and a horse trainer stealing away to Grenada after the trainer wrote a string of bad checks at racetracks. My boss wanted me to track down the jockey, visit him, and write about his life in the islands. And, oh, yes, I could take my wife along as well.

This is all I knew at the time: the jockey's name was Karl Korte, a well-known rider in the 1970s at thoroughbred tracks on the Pennsylvania–Maryland–New Jersey circuit. He was living in Grenada under an assumed name. So I called Grenada, asked an operator at a hotel there if anyone on the island had that name, and got through to him. He was eager to talk. He told me he was being held a virtual prisoner by a horse trainer named Elmer Eugene Zeek, who had been a friend, and with whom he had gone to Grenada. Now Korte wanted to return to the States, but was being held against his will. Zeek had become a business confederate of Grenada's prime minister, Sir Eric Gairy, and had the power to keep the jockey from leaving. Could I come down and talk to him, listen to his story, and then maybe tell the F.B.I. and get him out? He told me he was afraid to say anything more over the telephone.

Well, all of us in the newspaper business fantasize about being in an Indiana Jones kind of situation, don't we? Films and plays, especially *The Front Page* and Hitchcock's *Foreign Correspondent,* gave reporting a cachet, a life of excitement and danger. This story was somewhat different from night rewrite or a college soccer game. This was . . . what? Adventure.

Korte advised me to come to the island looking like a tourist. I bought a panama hat and dark glasses. The island was crawling with the prime minister's secret police. Gairy saw conspiracies everywhere. He once asked the United Nations to look into the issue of UFOs. Korte said it was a good idea for me to take my wife. I'd seem inconspicuous.

I know now the whole thing sounds ludicrous, if not dangerous. But Roz, my wife, has always looked for the amusing and exciting parts of assignments, and we raised our three children not to be surprised if all of us picked up and set off for anyplace, at any time. I always enjoyed having my family along on business trips—Stanley Cup playoffs, Super Bowls, championship fights. My wife taught the children there were no borders. However, this was one trip we thought they should avoid. We took them to Florida, dropped them off with Roz's parents, and went on to Grenada. We stayed at a Holiday Inn on the ocean, the beaches patrolled by soldiers carrying automatic weapons.

That night, Korte came to our room. He carried a pair of nunchakus—martial-arts sticks attached to chains, the kind you always see Bruce Lee whipping around his head. His story was theatrical, but gripping: how he was just an average jockey riding horses, and how Zeek, a successful trainer at the secondary tracks that dot the Northeast, had decided to get rich very quickly. Zeek habitually cashed checks for large sums of money at the tracks. So it was not unusual for, say, Penn National in Pennsylvania to give him forty thousand dollars in cash. That was all part of Zeek's scheme to pull a big one.

Over the extended Christmas holiday, Zeek cashed checks at various tracks totaling $1.4 million (back then, a million dollars was worth something). Because checks were processed by hand, it would take days—more than a week, considering the holiday—before the banks and tracks realized there was no money to cover the checks.

Korte told me that Zeek had investigated which countries had extradition treaties with the United States for the crime of wire fraud. Then Zeek went down the list to see which country had balmy breezes and might be a pleasant place to live. He hit upon Grenada. If he could escape there with his loot, he'd be safe.

Korte claimed he went along with Zeek because of a failed marriage, and a general sense of boredom as well as an attempt to put some excitement in his life. His description of the flight to Grenada was wonderful. It included a chartered Lear jet in which Zeek's girlfriend and her two huge Rottweiler dogs joined them. The dogs had diarrhea on the small plane during the flight.

But life got complicated once they got to Grenada. Zeek, who changed his name to Clancy, went into the duty-free liquor business with the prime minister. Then a fellow named Nicky showed up, a friend of Zeek's. Nicky also called himself Clancy and together they were the Clancy Brothers.

Now, as Korte related the story to us, he got extremely nervous and started to whisper. Nicky, it turns out, was wanted by everyone in the States—the mob, the feds. For Nicky was the prime witness to the Joey

Gallo murder that had been part of a series of gangland killings in New York. Nicky not only saw it but also had provided the gun to the hit man.

Joey (Crazy Joe) Gallo was gunned down in Little Italy at Umberto's Clam Bar, his favorite restaurant. The writer Jimmy Breslin described the hit this way: "Joey was having linguine in white clam sauce. After the bullets hit, Joey fell face down into red clam sauce."

Nicky needed a place to hide, and his pal Zeek offered him sanctuary on Grenada. They'd go in as brothers, partners with the nutty prime minister.

Korte wanted me to tell his story to the feds, who could figure out some way to get him off. He claimed Zeek watched him constantly and didn't want him to leave because he could testify against him in the States, which perhaps would lead to extradition on other charges.

"My paradise prison," said Korte, an engaging fellow who then gave Roz and I a demonstration of nunchakus in our motel room.

"I taught them to myself," he explained, "after watching Bruce Lee movies."

Korte also took out a handful of Chinese "stars," sharply pointed weapons that he had bought from a mail-order catalogue. The stars were tossed like a dagger. He took us outside and expertly sailed one into a tree, where it stuck fast.

But Karl cautioned me I could not write the story until he was safely back in the States. I thought that was fair. I also thought there was a heck of a book in this, and so I took out a sheet of hotel stationery, and in longhand wrote up an impromptu book contract if we were ever to meet again.

Then, Roz and I tried to get home. It was difficult to book flights in the Caribbean during Mardi Gras time, and I called the general manager I knew at a racetrack in Puerto Rico to use his influence with Eastern Airlines to get us back to Florida and pick up the children. I also told him the story.

We got on our flight from Grenada to San Juan. When we landed, we figured we'd be changing planes for Miami. Not so fast. Two men in suits approached us as we went through customs. They were F.B.I.

"We'd like to talk to you about Grenada," they said. Turns out, they were friendly with my acquaintance at the San Juan racetrack, and he told them the story—especially about Nicky.

"You said Nicky is there?" one of them asked. "He's the object of one of the biggest F.B.I. manhunts in the States. We don't like loose ends."

Anyway, we were debriefed, as they say. I told them everything I knew about Korte and Nicky and Crazy Joe Gallo. I also told them that Korte wanted to get off the island.

"I got an idea," one of the agents said. "We can't go into Grenada and take him out. It's a sovereign country. But maybe we can do something like this—get a seaplane. You and the pilot wait off shore, and Korte goes for a swim and then climbs aboard. You identify him, we fly him to Jamaica or some place we've got an embassy, which is considered American soil, and he's in U.S. custody."

That sounded great. The only thing is, I didn't think I'd get time off from the paper to do this undercover caper.

"Maybe you could send your wife," said the F.B.I. agent.

Actually, Roz sort of liked this idea. When she married me, she said she'd be in this newspapering adventure with me. Gotta leave tomorrow for L.A.? No problem. She'd pack up the kids and we were off. She learned something about every town I was ever in, and figured out ways to spend quality time there with the children. They were fearless together.

This is why my kids turned out the way they did, I think. Ellen has spectacular ideas in her C.E.O.'s role as an event planner in New York City. She married a traditional guy, Andy Shuster, a banker who knows more about sports than I do. Or maybe he just has more time to read statistics as he flies all over the country making deals. Mark, meanwhile, became a spine surgeon, a specialty that keeps him up late, yet out of the house before his wife, Anna, even pops out of bed and educates little children in a school. Luckily, she figured it would be like this when she met him. And Mike has climbed the Atlas Mountains in Morocco, studied film in Prague, explored Hollywood, did a stint at *Time,* and then made a difference advising the disadvantaged how to deal with government. Then he decided to go to law school.

This caper was different—my wife working with the F.B.I.! At least she gave it some thought. But when I brought it up with my editor, he said no—that we're not in the business of doing undercover work for the F.B.I.

Too bad. In any event, I had great stories for the children and my in-laws and mom and friends. I forgot about it after a few months at home. Korte and Company still were ensconced on the island. Then, I got an anonymous call in the office. Nicky was dead. That's all the caller told me. I phoned Grenada and learned that Nicky was found, face down, in a swimming pool. I called the coroner on the island.

"What was the cause of death?" I asked. "Drowning," said the coroner.

"How deep was the water?" I asked. "About two feet," was the reply.

Well, I wrote the story about Nicky's death for the paper. I got some independent confirmation about Nicky from the F.B.I. with the help of one of our reporters who specialized in organized crime. But the story didn't go into detail about Korte and Zeek. The paper felt it was extraneous. So that story had to wait. But when the story on Nicky's death appeared the next day, friends asked me if I was leaving sports to become a crime writer.

Some years passed, and one day I got a call. It was Karl Korte. He said that he was safely back in the States, living not far from me on Long Island with another horse trainer. Zeek had turned himself in and was doing time in prison. Korte wanted to get together with me for old times' sake. I promised to call him, but never did. The last time I read about him, he was a sixty-five-year-old exercise rider at small tracks. I really should give him a call.

When the grandchildren get a little older, I'll tell them this story. It will add to my mystique. Corey and Jane, and Alexa and Jordan already think I'm capable of extraordinary feats.

13

Money

Tempering adventure—indeed, so much of sports competition now—is the media's obsession with how much money everyone makes. It doesn't really seem possible now, does it, that athletes—these young, strong people making millions of dollars a year—were once no more than chattel? And the team sport that, more than any other, kept them restrained and locked into their team was hockey. That hardly seemed fair to me. It also didn't seem fair to sports agents. Why, some of them actually tried to negotiate with management—and for most of the twentieth century, anyone who did discovered management didn't want to negotiate with them.

This is the context I found myself in when I was writing hockey in 1968. Little by little, like peeling off an onion, I discovered layers of information about the sport that was kept from the general public as well as the players. One of these was something called the plus-minus statistic. It was quite important to coaches and general managers, yet many sportswriters were not even aware of it. Quite simply, it measured whether the opposition, or his own team, scored more goals while a player was on the ice. Many a player could be a prolific goal-scorer, but if his defensive play was so poor that more goals were scored against his team when he was playing, then he was a minus-player. Similarly, if while he was skating his team outscored the opposition, then he was a plus-player.

That seems like a simple enough statistic. But it was kept from the player, and the public. I was able to get this statistic, though, by calling the league's press office in Montreal, where an amiable fellow named Ron Andrews told me, "This is for your eyes only. You can use it, but you can't say where you got it from. Use it judiciously." I think Ron read too many James Bond books.

So every once in a while, if I needed it for a story, I'd use the number. Then one day I got a call from the agent of Vic Hadfield, one of the Rangers' stars.

"We need your help," the agent told me. "Vic says he can trust you. We have to find out Vic's plus-minus statistics." That's like a ballplayer who doesn't know his batting average calling a newspaper reporter to find out what it is. It's there, public record. Your own club can tell you that. Except in hockey, it wasn't public record. It was a secret.

"Francis won't give us the number," explained the agent, referring to the Rangers' coach–general manager, the redoubtable Emile Francis. He not only coached the team but also negotiated the players' salaries with them. It was quite a remarkable—and in the end, untenable—situation. On the one hand he had to praise them and prod them to play at their best as their coach; then when negotiating as their general manager he had to demean them. But that's the way hockey was back then—many coaches also were the general managers.

The agent said that Francis was claiming Hadfield was a minus-player while the two linemates he skated with, Rod Gilbert and Jean Ratelle, were plus. Thus, Francis was offering Hadfield considerably less money— if memory serves, thirty thousand dollars to their forty thousand—than the others.

Then the agent asked me, "Could you find out Vic's plus-minus figures?"

Well, I knew I could—but would I? Should I? I rationalized it for about six or seven seconds: it's not my job to help players get more money, I thought. Then again, all I really was doing was giving him statistical information. So I said yes. I called the league office, and again was admonished about the confidentiality of this factoid. Still, I passed it on. Hadfield and his agent were ecstatic. Francis had been juggling the true figure.

The funny thing about that plus-minus business is—nowadays it's routinely supplied by the league and published for anyone to see. Before every game everyone in the news media gets a team printout and every player's plus-minus figures are on there. Why the change? In 1972, a rival league, the World Hockey Association, came along. It was going to do things differently, and one of the changes was to bring hockey out of the Victorian era. It actually provided reporters in the press box with previously undisclosed figures such as a goalie's save percentage and a player's plus-minus figures, as well as how much ice-time a player logged. All these old-world secrets suddenly became public record. A bit of the mystique of hockey disappeared, but it opened a window allowing information to be viewed by everyone—not just miserly general managers hoping to put one over on their players.

These managerial excesses eventually blew up in ownerships' faces—in hockey and every other sport. Of course, it took more than unions to push up contracts: essentially, it took rival leagues. Thus, the sight of Bobby Hull receiving a one-million-dollar bonus check on the corner of Main and Portage Streets in Winnipeg as he jumped from the Chicago Blackhawks to the Winnipeg Jets. Or a fellow I wrote a book about, Derek Sanderson, leaving the Boston Bruins to leap to the new World Hockey Association. The book's subtitle was: "At 26 The World's Highest Paid Athlete."

That was actually true—for a few weeks. His annual salary in theory was $265,000. Today's inflation makes that less than the average hockey player's salary. Back then, though, it was more than ten times his salary with Boston. Derek never saw most of the projected money, even though he had bought a Rolls-Royce, in which he loved trying to pick up women at bus stops as he tooled around Philadelphia. He took me for a ride in the big car one day when we were working on his book.

"Look at this," he enjoyed showing me as he pressed a button and the window between the driver and the passengers went up. Eventually, Derek lost his money to profligacy ("He had an American Express credit card," his agent, Woolf, explained) as well as booze.

But within a year of the Hull and Sanderson dramatics, baseball free agency began in earnest when pitcher Dave Messersmith was able to break the bonds of the infamous reserve clause.

No one should be surprised that most sportswriters do not have a background in accounting, let alone economics. Thus many of my colleagues were sucked into all this new money talk and wrote about an endless spigot of wealth. In many ways it continues to this day: bandying about of "millions" of dollars. On closer inspection, some of these contracts merely are pieces of paper.

For example, even in the financially solid world of pro football, you routinely read about multiyear contracts in the millions. But virtually every contract in the National Football League has no guarantee covering the length of the contract. In other words, you may sign a deal worth, say, five million dollars over four years. But the club can cut you after one year. Or two years. The operative word is "potential." Contracts have "potential" values. In football, the only thing usually guaranteed is the signing bonus.

Of course, not all sports executives are miserly only with their players. Some are miserly with their spouses. I—or really, Roz, my wife—inadvertently may have played a role in a divorce settlement involving one of the world's wealthiest men.

Jack Kent Cooke was one of the more fascinating characters that sportswriting threw me into contact with. He owned New York's landmark Chrysler building—I mean, personally owned it. He also had another property—the Washington Redskins football team. Before that outfit, he had single-handedly owned both the Los Angeles Lakers basketball team and the Los Angeles Kings hockey team, as well as the arena they played in, the Forum (which actually was Greek-inspired). But Jack, a fastidious man, also was more interested in grandeur than historical accuracy.

I met him during the tumultuous talks in Montreal in 1965 that led to the NHL's expansion—it doubled in size from six to twelve teams. The league wanted to begin to share America's great and burgeoning television market, as well as to bring the sport to six major U.S. cities that had no major-league hockey.

Jack, who was born in Canada but who had become an American citizen through an act of Congress—he was an impatient man, and liked to use his clout—had set up shop in southern California. Cooke had been an extraordinary salesman in Canada, hawking soap and *Encyclopaedia*

Brittanica, before hooking up with the communications king who became known as Lord Thomson of Fleet. They ran various newspapers and television stations. In the States, Cooke made a second fortune as a pioneer in cable television.

Cooke, who also had been an executive in minor-league Canadian baseball, became a major U.S. sports figure as a prime force in the creation of the Continental League, a nascent outfit that threatened Major League Baseball's hold. His partner in the affair was a politically connected New York attorney named William A. Shea. The pair said their league would put a team in New York. That possibility forced Major League Baseball to create the New York Mets to prevent the arrival of a team from another league in the Big Apple. Shea wound up having a stadium named for him by a grateful city.

Cooke, meanwhile, retired to Pebble Beach, California. Bored at the age of fifty and without a job, he started acquiring sports teams. He put his old Canadian pal, Lorne Greene, star of the television show *Bonanza*, on the boards of directors. I had met Cooke briefly, and wrote an article describing how his former fellow Canadians were disgruntled with his big (un-Canadian) talk and boasts. He did not come off very well in my piece.

The next day, I was walking in a hotel lobby when Cooke spotted me.

"Jerry, my dear boy," he said, in tones that would make Stentor proud, "If I had realized you were writing for the *New York Times* I would have given you more time." He then asked me if I had read a book by a new author named Erich Segal. The book was *Love Story*, and Cooke liked it so much he autographed a copy and presented it to me.

I told him that I knew Segal. Erich, who taught classics at Yale, was a marathon runner, and I had written about him. I told Cooke I'd get Erich to give him a call. He did.

Anyway, Jack and I became acquaintances. I interviewed him from time to time. He left California, after divorcing his wife. The judge in California awarded his ex-wife a settlement that was the greatest in U.S. history at the time—forty-one million dollars, or a million dollars for each year of their marriage. The judge? His name was Wapner—he went on to a television career, presiding over *The People's Court*.

Fast-forward to 1983 and the Redskins are in the playoffs en route to

Super Bowl XVII. Cooke invited me to dinner at Duke Zeibert's restaurant in Washington. As usual, Jack got the table where he could see and be seen. Zeibert and Washington's elite figures passed our table, stopped and chatted. In the middle of dinner, during which my wife was describing her work with gifted children, Jack had an idea.

"My dear Rosalind," he said. "Maybe you can help me. I've got a car, this Jaguar, and it's acting funny. There's a light in it that won't go out. The electrical system is erratic. I've tried everything."

Roz asked him if he had driven the car to the restaurant. "It's right outside," he said. She asked him to get the owner's manual.

Jack was gone for a few minutes, and then brought in the booklet. My wife leafed through the index, found the page she wanted, and asked Jack if he had been turning the proper knobs.

"That's it!" he cried. "My darling, you are fantastic." He turned to me: "Jerry, where did you ever find such a woman?"

Some years later, I was watching the Phil Donahue show. The topic was about rich husbands who left their ex-wives impoverished. I recognized the woman Jack had been married to at the time we were in the restaurant together. She was his second wife.

"And what's your story?" Donahue asked her. "The only thing I got from my husband," she said, "is a fancy car that won't work right."

14

On the Road, from Po' Boys to Chateaubriand

When you arrive in a sports hotbed, you immediately become part of all the noise and hoopla. Yet as a journalist you are curiously disconnected. Your outsider status is punctuated by the fact that you cannot cheer, yet you are there because everyone in the setting is rabid for the team. That happened to me the first time I found myself in South Bend, Indiana, to do a story on Notre Dame football. Or when I went to Montreal to follow hockey's Canadiens. You get it in Dallas, for the Cowboys, at Yankee Stadium, in Green Bay for the Packers, old Boston Garden for the Celtics. It is all other-worldly, and yet you understand immediately. It sounds strange, I know, but some of that aura rubs off on you if you're a sportswriter. You feel a part of the championship history. In a sense, you are a part. You're writing about it—you are the link between observer and observed. But ultimately all you are is that link. You are neither fish nor fowl.

I had that feeling in Louisiana, in a woodsy part of a state that in no way is like my hometown. I was far from any big city. Yet I had come to Louisiana to write about Louisiana Tech's surprising men's basketball team and their star attraction, Karl Malone. I came to the state with an appreciation for at least a fictionalized version of its way of life.

I always tell students that in college, everything you'll study, everything you'll read, at some point in your life will be useful if you're a newspaper reporter. I tell them that physics or calculus will suddenly become helpful when you least expect it. I tell them about a story I wrote about the tires at the Indy 500, and that being a literature major didn't help me—but an overall liberal arts background did—when scientists from Goodyear were talking to me about the new speed rules regarding safety and tires.

Now, as I headed for Ruston, I thought about what I knew of Louisiana. And I kept coming back to the evocative novel I first read as a collegian, and that remains to this day a grand memory, and one of the books that made me glad I majored in literature: *All the King's Men.* The populist hero is adored by the average guy—much as the prototype Huey Long. Both overreached, and in the end the fictional hero is assassinated.

On my connecting flight through Baton Rouge, an elderly, frail man sat next to me in the bulkhead. Someone wheeled in his oxygen tank and set it beside him. He was, despite his infirmity, garrulous and outgoing, and soon we were talking about newspapers and basketball and the state of the world.

His name was Shady Wall, many times a millionaire thanks to Louisiana oil. And he could have been written as a character in the book by Robert Penn Warren. For all I know, he was. When we landed, he offered me a ride to the motel and dinner. He had a driver, he explained.

The chauffeur held open the door to a white Mercedes. I wondered where Wall planned to have dinner.

"I don't think there's anything open this late," he said. He saw a McDonald's. "Why don't you pull in here?" he told the driver. We went inside, with difficulty. The driver wheeled in the oxygen tank and we found a table in the back.

"Have you ever eaten here? I never have," Wall said. I told him to try the McNuggets. He dispatched his chauffeur to get them. I felt I was in some madcap 1930s movie, where the rich guy goes to the poor side of town and becomes one of the locals. Imagine being served by a chauffeur in a McDonald's.

"These are pretty good," said Wall after savoring his first McNugget.

I found out later he was one of the state's more popular political figures, a Democrat from Monroe who had helped to rewrite the Louisiana Constitution. He also was a true Louisiana Tech fan, a big financial supporter as well, and excited that I had come all the way from New York to write about his team.

The coach was a Chicagoan named Andy Russo, who was as much an anomaly in that part of the South as Malone might have been up north. For Malone was a 6-foot 9-inch junior whose mother couldn't stand to see him eating all that college food. So once a week she traveled from her home in Summerfield, while Malone drove from the campus. They'd stop halfway, each pulling over to the side of the road. He would give her a kiss and then she would haul out bags of groceries and chicken from her car. His mother was pleased. She had fed her growing son. This, of course, was so far from my own college experience as to seem almost fiction. You grow up in New York City with no comprehension of rural life. To the extent you think of it at all, it usually involves hayseed stereotypes from old movies. And yet, many years later when my children were in college, what did my wife and I do? We did just what Karl Malone's mom did. We brought them food—albeit, usually frozen.

I enjoyed talking with Malone, who had a sense of humor about what he was doing and what life was like at this school, its teams nicknamed the Bulldogs, that had until now been more famous for its women's team. He was only a junior, but was thinking of turning pro. He wondered what impact that would have on his teammates and the area. He knew that northwestern Louisiana had been famous for its quarterbacks—Terry Bradshaw, Joe Ferguson, and Bert Jones had made it to the NFL—and he knew he could be part of a different history. Still, the money to turn pro was inviting, he admitted.

Russo invited me to accompany the team to dinner. Everyone piled into a van. There was laughing and camaraderie and I had the sense this was going to be one of the last drives they all took together. The coach drove the van. This does not happen in many other colleges across America, I thought.

My foray into deepest Louisiana lasted only a few days. But I followed the team and its fortunes when I returned home. It didn't capture a championship. Soon, Malone opted to turn pro instead of going into his senior year, and enjoyed one of the longest and most successful careers in NBA history. Russo also left Louisiana Tech and went to a major-college program at Washington, and then on to other schools.

Shady Wall died a few years later. When I heard that he had died, I felt genuine sadness, for he and the group of people I had written about had become much more than simply people living in a vacuum, another story to be pounded out. They had become real people, with aspirations so like mine, or like players from New York University or Notre Dame.

Although none of my New York friends has ever heard of Louisiana Tech, and knows little of the state except what they've heard about New Orleans, I think about my time in that corner of America, and how there is a big world out there. Writing allowed me to enter another part. I think I'm going to the library to reread *All the King's Men*.

I never grew too jaded to appreciate the nuances and surprises of the road. Next to the beguiling idea of spring training, going on the road is the great allure for young sportswriters. In my case, I was twenty-four years old before I had ever gone as far as Boston from Brooklyn.

Imagine, though: newspapers actually paid for a reporter to travel— to great cities, usually, for that was where the action was, where major-league teams competed. The first trip I took for the *Times,* the overnighter in 1964 to Boston and my first hockey game, was hardly glamorous. But I found out the paper paid my cab fare to LaGuardia airport. I could even be reimbursed for newspapers in the coffee shop. I could charge for meals, for tips, for phone calls. I could eat whatever I wanted. And I was having fun just doing my job.

I learned, too, that if four of us shared a cab, we'd still be able to charge our offices for the price of a cab ride. "Four receipts, please," was the sportswriters' joke about taking a cab to the game.

I had been a reporter about two years when I was asked to cover the Stanley Cup finals between the Montreal Canadiens and Chicago Black-hawks. The series opened during Easter, when my wife was off, along with her students in a New York City school. So for the first time, Roz and I went on the road together—from Montreal to Chicago. In Chicago, we stayed at the Bismarck Hotel, an old-world establishment that made sensational Wiener schnitzel. The hotel was owned by Jim Norris, one of the sports world's wealthiest men (his family fortune came from shipping along the Great Lakes). Norris, though, also was fascinated with boxing, and was head of the most important fight organization in America—Madison Square Garden's boxing club. He also owned the

Chicago Blackhawks and their stadium. Norris's boxing connections were suspect, as was most of the fight game in the 1950s and 1960s. Indeed, because of mob affiliations, his boxing empire was broken up by the government, which charged it had an octopuslike grip on the sport all over America.

Norris also owned racehorses, and so he coyly named one "Octopus." Take that, feds.

I interviewed him after one hockey practice, and asked him what he'd been doing since he had been stripped of his boxing business. "Well, Jerry, I'm not exactly bored," he said. "I've got some other things going on."

That night, my wife and I were having dinner in the Bismarck, and I noticed Norris sitting at a nearby table with his wife. They did not speak during dinner. At one point, he asked a waiter to bring him a pack of cigarettes. The waiter handed the pack to Norris. Norris looked at the pack, then the waiter—and wordlessly returned the pack. Something had been breached, I thought. Of course, I quickly realized: etiquette, involving this man with the mobster fascination.

The maitre d' realized what had happened. He rushed over to the table, took the pack of cigarettes out of the waiter's hands and, with a withering glance at the waiter, tapped a cigarette from the pack, and offered it to Norris. Then the maitre d' whipped out his own lighter, and lit Norris's cigarette. Norris never blinked.

I still see that image of the couple, Norris and his wife, sitting eerily silent over dinner—nothing to say. But whatever else was going on in his personal life, Norris was royalty in that restaurant.

Roz couldn't remain with me the entire hockey series since the Easter break ended before the finals did. I went back to Montreal with the Canadiens, who traveled by train. I had befriended the Canadiens' press relations director, Camil des Roches, an amiable little man with a perfect brush mustache. Camil was flattered that the *Times* had sent a reporter to cover the finals.

"I learned English by reading the *Times*," Camil explained, quite proudly. He arranged for me to interview the Canadiens' star, Jean Beliveau, on the trip between Chicago and Montreal.

Beliveau was a most elegant player—a willowy center who skated with grace and who epitomized the Gallic flair of the Canadiens hockey team. Beliveau knocked on the door to my compartment and introduced himself. He was wearing a blue suit, white shirt, and blue tie. He was about 6 feet 2 inches tall, and obviously uncomfortable in my little suite, but he sat down and told me about his life. He had replaced a Canadiens' icon—really, the Babe Ruth of hockey—in Maurice (Rocket) Richard. In Beliveau's formal English and lilting French-Canadian accent, he admitted, "Whatever I did after him was never enough. If I scored one goal they wanted two. If I scored three, they wanted four."

And yet, Beliveau was considered hockey's finest player at the time. Still, he recalled his early days and the impossibility of following a legend. It was the first in-depth interview I had with an athlete, and it taught me to search for the human side of the star—that everyone had a story to tell if you could plumb it correctly. I spent much of the next forty years searching for more Beliveaus.

Because many of my stories appeared in the *Toronto Globe and Mail,* which subscribed to the *Times*'s news service, I was making a name for myself in Canada. So during a Rangers' road trip to Toronto in the late 1960s, I was invited on a *Firing Line*-style television show with several Canadian writers. The guest we were to quiz was Arthur Ashe. Arthur was the world's top tennis player. He also was soft-spoken, but very much in command. I thought we all were going to have a nice and easy conversation about playing the gentlemanly sport of tennis. After all, Ashe was an amateur. The pro game had not taken hold.

"How long have you been taking money under the table?" the host asked to kick off the show. Arthur, who also was an officer in the army and wearing his uniform, never blinked. He calmly described the way tennis worked. I don't think I got in a question—or, if I did, it certainly wasn't an accusatory statement. When the show ended, Arthur asked if I'd like to share a cab with him. I had never met him before.

We spoke about Vietnam in the cab, spoke about journalism, spoke about the grilling he had just taken. Nothing fazed him.

Often, when you meet a person who is more than an athlete—who has become a symbol as well—the temptation is to want to go beyond the mundane. I wanted to talk to Ashe about the big picture of race in America, about his role, about . . . well, a taxi ride isn't the place to suddenly ask such a major question. And anyway, I'm sure in almost every interview he gave, Ashe was asked to address issues beyond the immediate. So I said good-bye to him feeling unfulfilled, sensing that an important moment had escaped me. It was another lesson I learned—you don't always get second chances to ask questions. I never ran across him again.

If something needs to be asked, don't wait. Of course, I'm still not sure what I would have asked him. If I asked him about race, would that mean that all I saw him as was a black man in a white man's game? Perhaps I should be grateful that I had the opportunity to take a ride with Arthur Ashe in a taxi in Toronto, and that we had a pleasant conversation. Wouldn't a lot of people like to say that they had, too?

Once upon a time, before sports became complicated and much of management and many of the players openly distrusted us, we used to travel together. It went back to baseball days and the sleeper cars on the railroad. Routinely, writers had their upper or lower berths not far from the ballplayers. They ate together in the dining car, drank and smoked together in the club car.

There was a somewhat different version when I started to cover the Jets in 1975—they, of course, traveled by jet, and charter jet at that. I traveled with them for thirteen years, and it was always an exciting experience—in some ways like a gala departure on a cruise ship. Well, maybe no one popped open the champagne, but there always was a sense of adventure unfolding, especially if the Jets were playing well.

On the flights, there was an unwritten code for the press—let the players drink up in the back, where many of them had their little flasks stashed in carry-on bags (we always sat in first class, with the coaches), and don't write about boisterous behavior. For the most part, we held to that code, although we also were permitted to walk around and interview players.

But the most important aspect of this gala experience was Namath. Until rock stars and their hangers-on and their desire for elaborate security came along, it is doubtful if any other celebrity ever was ushered in and out of planes quite the same way. Hundreds of people waited for Joe outside the stadium after road games. There always was a private security guard on his floor at the team hotel. Phone calls to his room went to his agent, who traveled with him.

The club's traveling secretary was a folksy, genial southerner named John Free. John loved to regale us late at night with the ways he spirited Joe aboard a plane and avoided riots. There was a moment in San Diego, where the locker room opened onto a tunnel. When Free peered down to the end of it, he saw a mob waiting around the team buses. Free had been dealing with this phenomenon for years—when the Jets captured Super Bowl III in 1969, Joe had become a walking (albeit gimpily) legend. Free saw the San Diego Chargers' laundry van loading towels. He approached the driver. "I'll give you ten dollars if you drive this gentleman out of the stadium, park a block away, and wait for me." The driver looked at Free and the passenger, said, "That's Joe Namath. OK."

There was one complication. The driver's girlfriend was along for the ride. She was sitting on the bundles of towels in the back. And Joe was probably America's most notorious bachelor.

"Come up front with me," the driver told his girlfriend. "Namath can stay in the back with the towels by himself. I don't want you sitting back there with him."

Thus was the great Joe Namath spirited out of the stadium in a laundry truck.

Even after Joe no longer was a Jet, the team still had a sense of excitement about it. We always had a motorcycle escort whisking us from airport to hotel, hotel to airport. When Joe Walton coached the team in the 1980s, he liked to sit on the aisle in the first bulkhead. He could see everyone coming in. I often sat on the aisle opposite Joe. But that first seat is the coach's prerogative in every sport I've ever seen—on the buses as well. Joe and his fellow coaches could check on the condition of each player, and also be alert for someone who has gotten on who doesn't belong.

That actually happened on a Jets' flight before the age of super-tight security. Before leaving Oakland, where strange Raiders fans paint their bodies and act sort of nuts, Free was walking through the aisle on the charter flight, making sure everyone who was there belonged. One guy didn't. He had sneaked on. Free said nothing, but walked over to one of his jumbo linemen and told him to sit next to the intruder.

Then Free inquired of the stowaway, gently, just what the heck he was doing on a Jets' charter flight. "I heard you guys were going to New York, and I needed a ride, so I figured I'd get on," he explained.

I guess if I were a fan I would have been ecstatic to be airborne with a pro team. It was something like a party, with grandmotherly hostesses. The flight attendants really wanted this assignment because it was easier to work—you had perhaps eighty passengers instead of two hundred, and because the attendants had to stay on the road overnight, union rules decreed they were amply compensated. Thus, the flight attendants who worked the Jets' jets usually were the senior people, many with thirty years in, and with their choice of assignments. They babied the players from the time they went up the steps, when they were plied with soda, beer, and chips.

The "stewardesses," as they were known in that earlier time, often wore Jets' jerseys over their blouses. They were continually working the aisle handing out candy bars or apples. One of the airline's managers, who always accompanies a pro team, told me that where the playful Jets were concerned, "I'd never have grapes or bananas on board. With football players, if they had grapes, they'd throw them." One of the team's owners, Helen Dillon, once brought aboard a birthday cake for defensive lineman Marty Lyons. Players ran their fingers through the whipped cream and smeared one another.

While all of this sounds nifty to the average person, two unusually successful coaches—indeed, each with Super Bowl credentials—hated flying so much it played a role in their quitting the game.

The most famous nonflyer in sports is John Madden, who has become the best-known broadcaster in football. I wish I could say I convinced him to fly again. He won a Super Bowl with the Raiders, but quit football because of the constant pressure he felt whenever he flew. And West Coast teams always log more air miles than any other clubs. As a broadcaster, he is still noted for his refusal to fly. He has had as many stories written about his travels on his famous customized bus—in which two drivers propel him about from game to game, north to south, east to west—as about his broadcasting ability. We were sitting over lunch somewhere—probably a Super Bowl—and I gingerly brought up the subject of flying. I understood Madden's fear.

In the spring of 1965, when I landed at LaGuardia after a flight from Montreal, my wife told me she was pregnant with our first child. I still don't know what triggered my reaction—I understand that significant events in a person's life can do that—but I did not fly for the next ten years.

I explained to Madden how I slowly had worked my way back to flying through a form of behavioral therapy—I actually hired a helicopter and pilot. We were on a helicopter pad alongside the Hudson River. We'd go up twenty feet—then thirty feet. The moment I felt any discomfort, we would go lower. Then we'd cross the Hudson to Staten Island or New Jersey and return. A five-minute ride. I'd tell the pilot to take it to the height at which I felt comfortable. From helicopters, I went on to private planes, hiring off-duty commercial airline pilots to whisk me on ten-minute trips, usually little more than takeoffs and landings. I discovered there was a scheduled flight on a major airline from Long Island to Connecticut that lasted seven minutes. I took it. Whatever the reason, this strategy worked, and I went back to flying and now cannot imagine having to go by train.

I told this to Madden—not suggesting he do the same, but merely to show that this was possible and how I handled it. He listened without ever giving me a hint of how he felt, whether this was a possibility for him, whether he was upset over his inability to fly. He displayed no interest in flying, or even asked me any questions about my own return. When he got up to leave, I told him if he ever wanted to discuss it, I'd enjoy talking to him further. He still hasn't called.

Even more surprising than Madden's reaction to flying was learning that the remarkable Bill Parcells will fly only if it means he can't get to a game otherwise. Parcells is perhaps the preeminent coach in the NFL. His Giants teams captured two Super Bowls. He led the Patriots to a Super Bowl appearance. He took over a laughingstock Jets franchise and brought the team to within a pass or two of a Super Bowl appearance. He soon left the Jets for television, then unretired again to take over football's iconic team, the Dallas Cowboys.

He is a controlling, often maddening, personality. He also is one of the smartest and most fascinating people I have ever been around. But one day we were talking about a trip I had taken to Africa. I told him about the safaris and he was intrigued. I knew he had a host of interests, and was curious about the way everyone did his job, how grass grew on football fields, how animals reacted—in short, how the natural world behaved.

I told him, "You'd love Africa."

Bill Parcells and me during Super Bowl week in January 1991.

"Nah," he said. "How long does it take to get there?" I told him it was about a fifteen-hour flight. He looked at me as if I were nuts. He shook his head.

"You'd never get me on a flight that long. I hate to fly." Then he explained that the constant anxiety he had over flying had been one reason—he also had serious health concerns—he had left the Giants eight years earlier and had taken a television job rather than return to coaching. This was a man in such control, who always exuded confidence, who never wavered from decisions—even when they were wrong—but had limited the things he could do because of one aspect of his life he could not master.

As for me, when I resumed flying, I went on to travel all over the world. I got interested in wine, in food, in exploring, and learned there was a writer's market for stories on some aspect of every trip I have taken. I had virtually been handed this unique opportunity. Mostly, it was all for fun, and I have had as much enjoyment traveling as writing about sports, or wine, or safaris.

Take my moment on the stage at the Grand Ole Opry. Yes, that was my wife and I you might have seen in the wings that November night in 1998.

The Jets were playing the Tennessee Titans, a perfect opportunity to explore Nashville with my wife, who had retired two years earlier, and who had started to accompany me on whirlwind three-day road trips to interesting cities—fly out on a Friday night after I wrote my stories for the Saturday and Sunday paper, have all day Saturday to be tourists, then go out to dinner on Sunday night after a game, and fly back to New York on Monday. It was the Captain's Paradise, except I brought along my wife.

Naturally, I called some people at the Opry and asked about seeing the show on Saturday night. Better yet, I was told, why don't I come a few hours earlier and visit backstage? Why, sure.

Until that day, I had barely been aware of someone named Vince Gill. I think I might have heard the Opry as a child when I played with the radio dial, and something tells me I remember Minnie Pearl shouting "Howdee!" Maybe not. Maybe I just read about it.

We got to the Opry about two hours before showtime and a public relations person told me, "You can hang out here if you want." "Here" was a few feet from the stage. There was no hustle nor bustle as musicians and singers and performers simply walked about. In fact, an hour before the show, I saw no performers. It was all rather off-handed.

About fifteen minutes before the show a big, amiable guy—looking like a former high school quarterback—came alongside us. "Hi," he said. He had a guitar in his hands. "Vince Gill," he said, extending a hand. I introduced myself and my wife, and when he found out I was a sportswriter, started to talk golf. He knew about the Jets. He was a sports fan. I wish I could have told him I loved his newest album. I had no idea what songs he'd sung.

He told me he hadn't been booked on the show until Thursday. "When did you rehearse?" I asked. "Oh, we don't rehearse here," he said. He explained that the musicians all knew his songs. But what about the back-up singers? I wondered. "They know the music, too," he said. "They're pretty good." "You mean, you just show up?" I asked.

He laughed. "That's about it. Well, got to go on now. Nice meeting you."

While he was on, a grandmotherly type sauntered over to us. She had a little dog with her. She introduced herself: "Jeannie Seely." I didn't know it, but it turned out she had been the first woman to host the Opry. Now she was a fixture, so comfortable there she showed up with her dog. When I told her we were visiting from New York, she asked how we liked Nashville, what we thought of the Opry, what our plans were for the rest of the trip.

We might have been a couple of out-of-towners, but a pair of country music superstars treated us like kin. I never got a reception like that in the Yankees' clubhouse.

I started taking my children along on road trips in the late 1960s, when I'd head up north, to Kitchener, in the fall to write about the Rangers' hockey training camp. It lasted more than a week, and I had some free time. In the clear Canadian autumn, we'd drive into neighboring towns, visit the London (Ontario) Fair, or the antiques shops of St. Agatha. At night, we ate in the formal, old-world restaurant of the Hotel Wolper. It was a German-style establishment, not surprising, since Kitchener had been called "Berlin" before World War I.

We enjoyed in particular the welcoming ways of an elderly waiter. He had a mittel-European accent and seemed to enjoy describing the food and wine. One evening I asked him to try some wine I thought had turned bad. He demurred. "I used to be the sommelier here," he explained, then added with some sadness, "but my nose went bad."

Thus, he was demoted to being a waiter. That was the way they did it in Europe in the old days, I guess. I remember that moment more than I remember any of the Rangers' training-camp activity.

The road became more fun for my children when they got older. I began taking the entire family along on Super Bowl trips. The parties were a spectacular lesson for Ellen, who went on to make some remarkable galas in New York in her event-planning company. And once a year I'd take one of the children with me on a road game. One such occasion brought me to Atlanta with my youngest, Mike, who was fourteen years old.

Many years earlier, I had been to a restaurant outside of town named

Aunt Fanny's Cabin. It was housed in a former slaves' quarters, and had become a landmark run by black ownership. I played tour director and made arrangements for a dozen writers, along with Mike, to go there on a Saturday night.

They served every dish in the southern lexicon of food, and played great jazz as well. While we were enjoying dessert, and a rendition of "St. James Infirmary," Mike turned to me and said, "You know, Dad, you've got a great job."

I thought about it—this was one of those golden moments with your child when you can assess your life. He was right. It took my son to remind me of it.

Funny, but thirty years earlier, when I was just starting, I had that similar feeling, that this business I was getting into would be filled with many warm moments. It happened at another retirement party of the paper's old guard. The reporter's name was Roscoe McGowen, who had been a baseball writer for decades.

It was at an upstairs room at a Midtown restaurant, maybe Sardi's. I heard a tinkling piano, around which several writers were standing, holding their drinks. One of the reporters was another old-timer, Joe Nichols. He was the boxing and horse-racing writer and he had an eclectic circle of friends. One of these was the gray-haired man playing the piano. He played a few unfamiliar bars of the verse to a song, and then went into the more familiar chorus. I knew it immediately, and so did everybody else. It was "Tea for Two."

"Jerry, this is Irving Caesar. He wrote it," Nichols said to me. Caesar nodded and smiled. I sang along, holding my drink, noticing there were other glasses on the piano, and wondering how many more moments in my budding newspaper career would equal this—singing "Tea for Two" with the fellow who wrote it.

Interesting, isn't it, that so many newspaper stories still revolve around booze? I think these are diminishing. I recall one that seemed perfect for the time and place.

This is another memory from the Lake Placid Winter Olympics of 1980. We had a free night, and so Red Smith, Dave Anderson, Jack Murphy (who had the stadium in San Diego named for him because he wrote so many newspaper columns badgering politicians to build one) and I went out for dinner at a Chinese restaurant named Chopstix. Murph and Red were two of the grand old names in the business. They told wonderful stories that night as their faces got redder and the liquor flowed.

The restaurant was distinguished for an oddity: it only had mu shu beef to go. They wouldn't serve it to me in the restaurant. So I ordered it to go, and ate it there.

After dinner Dave and I dropped off the two old-timers. Smith and Murphy were sharing a room in one of those old wooden motels that had a set of antlers over the door. They were staggering a bit as they went inside. I waited about ten minutes and knocked on the door to see if they were OK.

I went inside and saw the two gentlemen: Each wore pajamas, each was in his bed, covered up to his neck with a blanket. And each was holding a martini in his right hand.

It was perfect. I told Dave I thought it was all right to leave.

There are some cities sportswriters should pay their own way to—Seattle, San Francisco, and New Orleans come to mind.

Imagine: the *Times* gave me an expense account to go to restaurants, sample beignets, visit jazz joints, to do a story about parties in New Orleans during Super Bowl week of 1981. The national news desk wanted a firsthand account of the kinds of places visitors were going to, as well as the more sophisticated haunts. Although I had been to New Orleans several times before, I needed some guidance in this area. Luckily for me, two of my cousins, Michael and Phil Dinhofer, were attending Tulane University's law school. Armed with *Times* money, I told them to show me around.

First, we started out with dinner at a place I had heard about, but that was not yet nationally recognized—K-Paul's, a restaurant run by a serious, and very heavy, man named Paul Prudhomme. He was to bring Cajun cooking into mainstream American kitchens, first with his blackened redfish, then blackened steak (soon, everything on American menus and even every Greek-owned diner seemed to be "blackened"), and ultimately with his Cajun approach to cuisine. He wound up with his own television show, too, and became one of America's celebrity chefs.

My friend Dick Schaap, the television and publishing personality, introduced me to Prudhomme, who gave me a tour of his kitchen. It was a chore for him to get around. He was a man of imposing girth who was happier sitting down and having people come to him and praise his food.

While I was eating, I'd take out my reporter's pad and make notes—not sentences, but a few catchwords that would, when I looked at them later, jog my memory and allow me to recount, in faithful detail, what had unfolded earlier. It was a trick I had learned interviewing people. Early on, I realized that unless I learned shorthand, I'd never be able to transcribe quotes exactly. I'd spend so much time writing what people said that I wouldn't be able to finish scribbling one sentence before the next began. I learned I was able, however, to put down an important phrase, and if the subject were switched to something I wanted to continue to write about, a word or two would bring back the context, if not the exact quote.

Of course, as the years went by, the tape recorder became a staple of interviewing. Every writer I've come across who started in the business since the 1980s uses a tape recorder. I've used one, too, in writing books, for the person I'm writing about has gotten to know me well enough so that he doesn't feel self-conscious or constrained by the little gadget. And there are so many thousands of words you need in a book that a tape recorder is a required tool.

But the problem with a tape recorder in daily journalism, especially in sportswriting, I believe, is that it puts an artificial layer between you and the subject. An exception is a news conference, in which several people are asking questions and the subject often is at a desk or podium that has many tape recorders on it, or is speaking into a microphone. But if I had put one of those little voice-activated tape recorders in front of, say, John Denver, whose table I found myself at during one Super Bowl involving the Broncos, I don't think our conversation would have been as free and easy.

So in that New Orleans restaurant, as we sat and had a fine old time, I didn't want to ruin the mood by taking out my notepad—and I certainly wouldn't put a tape recorder on a table with the clatter of dishes and silverware and conversation. I simply wrote down a few words that I knew would be meaningful later. I looked at my notes later. All I had jotted was "blackened redfish."

That night, though, we were three kids out on the town. We did the touristy but still fun Bourbon Street, stopped in Pat O'Brien's, where my cousins got some "hurricanes" and we heard the pianist play "Tin Roof Blues." We got to Preservation Hall, where I bribed the band with an extra five dollars to hear them play the "Saints," then headed over to Tchoupitoulas Street in uptown New Orleans, near Tulane, where we sipped Dixie Beer out of the bottle at Tipitina's bar and watched inter-racial couples dancing to an accordionist playing Cajun two-step music.

At times, I forgot that I was working. My notepad stayed in my pocket. Then I'd suddenly remember what I was there for, whip it out, and try to write in some darkened corner of a bar where people were jostling my elbows. Ah, what we do for our art.

My son Mike was right. It's a great job. I had so much fun that night I would have paid for it myself. Not surprisingly, I got that story about what people were doing for enjoyment in New Orleans. How could I miss?

15

Do-Overs

One of the difficulties I have had in my forty-something years is balancing what I perceived as my paper's disinclination to offend, and to avoid controversy. Too often, I wound up taking a straight-and-narrow approach. I am trying to atone for these misdeeds now.

Two incidents stand out, both involving college basketball.

There was a tournament at Madison Square Garden. One of the games involved New York University and Villanova. NYU was a melting-pot school in America's melting-pot city. Villanova was a Catholic school.

At college basketball games everywhere you always hear screaming put-downs, especially during free-throw shooting by the opposition. But during one confrontation on the floor, in which there was a bit of pushing and shoving, some of the Villanova fans began chanting, "Arm the Arabs!" The message was clear to me. It was anti-Semitic. How else to interpret this? This wasn't a political rally. It was a game involving a predominantly Jewish school, and at the first sign of conflict, some of the Villanova students picked up the obvious religious angle.

I called the copy desk. I was told I could use the quote in my story, but not make an issue of it. Somewhere in the middle of my piece I had the Villanova fans screaming "Arm the Arabs!" Nothing more. Today, for better or for worse, that would be the lead.

Several years later I covered a game at St. John's, in Jamaica, Queens, involving Creighton University of Omaha. Their star was a Jew from

New York City. I had heard shouting directed at him during the game, followed by laughter. When the game ended, I went up to him in the locker room. He was crying. He explained that some of the fans had called him anti-Semitic names.

My story simply detailed "cruel slurs." Perhaps I was leery of making it seem Catholics were anti-Semitic. Several readers, though, called me in the morning and asked the nature of those insults. They seemed to figure it out. Ironically, our assistant sports editor, Joseph M. Sheehan, whose brother was a priest, asked me, "Why didn't you say they were ethnic insults?"

That taught me: write it, then let the copy desk argue about changing something. But go with your instincts on what's right. Don't be cowed by the sensibilities of the publication, or the public.

What about the sensibilities of a person, though? Many famous athletes have well-documented domestic problems. But what if you know them? And what if detailing them has questionable newsworthiness? I think of two transcendental athletes I knew, and of something I knew about them. I can raise the issues now because their stories have come out, although the majority of the public may not be aware of them.

Joe Namath was transformed once he retired. At the age of forty-one he finally got married. I had contemplated doing a book with him, and we agreed to talk on the set of *Kate and Allie,* the television sit-com. He was doing a guest appearance. He talked incessantly of his wife, Deborah, and his daughter. Everywhere he went on business, he said, they went, too. He turned down many appearances if he couldn't bring them with him.

I wrote a piece about how Joe, once America's bachelor, had become America's husband and daddy.

A few years later, I ran into him at an airport. He invited me to play golf when I got to Florida. Then he took out a piece of paper and said, "Here's my wife's name and the girls' names, so if they answer the phone you'll know who you're speaking to." A nice gesture, I thought.

I looked at the piece of paper. Under his wife's name he wrote "Tatiana."

"Tatiana?" I thought. "Wasn't her name Deborah?" Had he gotten divorced? I wondered.

I phoned a mutual friend, who related this story: Deborah, who was considerably younger than Joe, had never really liked her given name. She was named for a cousin who had died a few weeks before she was born. Now Deborah was approaching her thirtieth birthday. "Before you're thirty," Joe told her, "why don't you change your name to something you like?" Deborah liked that idea. But to what? She happened to be reading a Russian novel. She came across the name Tatiana. So that was it.

When I heard that story, I phoned Joe. I told him I thought it was a wonderful anecdote, and I'd like to use it in a book I was writing about the Jets called *Gang Green*.

"I'd appreciate it if you didn't use it," said Joe. "It's really sort of personal." I went along with him.

But then, a year later, Tatiana left him. I heard that she had gone to Hollywood, that she had always been interested in trying to get into show business. I also heard that she had found a younger man. Within another year, she in fact did divorce Joe, and took the two girls to live with her in California. Joe was depressed, but tried to spend as much time with the girls as he could.

How ironic that sport's most famous bachelor of the 1960s—really, a symbol of the new wave of young players—was left by his younger wife. I had been concerned about breaking a confidence in writing about "Tatiana." In none of the stories I read about the divorce did I see any mention of Tatiana's real first name.

Another icon of the sixties was hockey's Bobby Hull, known as "The Golden Jet." In the days before helmets were mandatory, Hull's billowing blond hair punctuated his soaring skating style, which featured the hardest slap shot the game had known. He also was one of the most gracious athletes I had come across, willingly staying after games to hand out autographs to fans, and patiently listening to reporters' questions. He had once told me how he had cried himself to sleep as a youngster playing junior hockey 150 miles from home, and how important it was for him to raise a family.

Bobby came to New York to be honored for his contributions to the NHL. Before the dinner he held court with several reporters. I remarked that he seemed tired.

"Well, my wife is pregnant," he said. "And you know, when the cat's away, the mice will play."

It was, of course, a gross, wiseass comment. It had no place in the hockey story I was writing for the next day's paper. But it stunned me because of his lack of propriety, his good-old-boy wink.

Some years later, his wife divorced him and held a public auction of many of his trophies and awards. She actually threw some of them into the street, including a most valuable player trophy and a Stanley Cup championship blanket. Many writers were shocked by the severity of her anger toward him, and how she embarrassed this Hall of Famer. It served him right, I thought.

In retrospect, I should have been more outraged in writing about a group of other athletes—although not about them so much as their parents, and the system that virtually encouraged a loss of childhood. There are two particularly insular worlds in sports—figure-skating and gymnastics, both dominated by women—that journalists have smoothed over. I don't think it is intentional. I think that, like most things we do in daily journalism, we write about the surface, what we see. But in these two sports in particular, and which draw the most number of women as television viewers, something important has been missing—a look at their dark sides.

Dorothy Hamill had captured three U.S. figure-skating championships by the time she was nineteen years old, in 1976, when I interviewed her. Her mother sat nearby, in a protective mode, as we spoke. Matter-of-factly, Dorothy told me she practiced seven hours a day, six days a week, for eleven months. She was from Connecticut, but had moved to Denver while in high school so she could be near her coach. She said she saw her brothers for two days once a year, at Christmas. When she was sixteen years old, she told me, she started to throw up from anxiety before performing.

It all seemed outrageous to me—almost child abuse (an expression hardly in vogue back then). And yet, my story was more of a gee-whiz piece, how hard this young woman worked. Harder, I wrote, than the icons of that day, Jack Nicklaus or Kareem Abdul-Jabbar or Billie Jean King, practiced their skills.

How sad that almost thirty years after the interview, after a story that

Bobby Hull, playing for the Chicago Blackhawks in 1967. Courtesy of the John Halligan Collection.

detailed the excruciating practice routines that she had put her body through, Dorothy Hamill now was doing commercials for Vioxx—the medicine for arthritis sufferers. Yet we in the business understood there was something wrong with much of what we were watching, but rarely if ever outraged the public with stories that might have helped these youngsters.

Similarly, I had seen this intense work schedule for young gymnasts. One day I was at West Point doing a piece on an Olympic-qualifying event for women—actually girls, since women are over the hill in gymnastics once they leave their teen years.

By then Olga Korbut had become an international figure for her daunting skills in the Olympics, which hundreds of millions of television viewers had seen worldwide. She was followed as the premier gymnast by another tiny celebrity, Nadia Comaneci. These Munchkinlike figures were the role models for the new generations of female gymnasts who gathered around television sets, or attended the performances.

Now, at West Point, as I watched in person American teenagers go through their tricks (as they are called) and routines, it seemed odd: they all had the bodies of a prepubescent nine- or ten-year-old. Every last one of them. Even fifteen-year-olds. Then I thought of Korbut and Comaneci. If you were to see them in a high school class, you would have thought them deformed, or malnourished.

I wondered why no one had ever pointed that out, in newspapers or television coverage. Was there something in gymnastics that did this, or was there a natural selection—you needed this sort of body to become good? I was sitting at the press table, next to an official of the U.S. Gymnastics Federation. I said to him, "Why do these teenagers all have the bodies of little kids?"

He smiled defensively. "That is a sensitive area in gymnastics," he said. "It's there, but we don't talk too much about it."

I did a little reading about the subject when I returned home. This constant battering of young bodies affects the hormonal switches that control aspects of sexual development, I learned. The intense and constant workouts at such an early age—most started when they were pre-teens—delayed the onset of womanly development.

I blew a story. But then again, I wasn't there to write an exposé. And the Olympics weren't my beat. But I know now that I certainly should have pointed out to my editor that there was an important story to write. Yet figure skating and gymnastics and who knows how many other sports have escaped the glare of journalists, who instead jump on the story of grown men who take steroids to bulk up, or ephedra to lose weight.

16

Deep Ghost

Having my name in the paper, and meeting so many athletes and club officials and fans, allowed me to complement my newspaper writing. It led me to write fourteen books, including this one. I have ghost-written books in collaboration with Hall of Fame baseball players Willie Mays and Carl Yastrzemski; with hockey Hall of Famer Phil Esposito and Derek Sanderson; I have written books about baseball maverick Bill Veeck and baseball manager Leo Durocher.

All were easy—to a point. That point was the money advance—once it came in, I learned you had to tie the players down to get them to sit. And as for the deceased Veeck and Durocher—well, naturally, many of the people who knew them were concerned that their legends not be altered. Arriving at the truth of someone you have never met is daunting. It reminded me of the Indian legend of the blind men confronting an elephant. One person grabbed the trunk and said it was a giant snake. Another stroked the feet and thought it was a tree.

Of all the subjects, Mays had the most legendary status. He was a true American icon, famed as much for his exuberance as his spectacular play—he could run, hit, field. The images of him were pure Americana baseball: hat flying off as he rounded second base, chasing a fly ball, playing stickball in the streets of Harlem as a rookie.

I was surprised one day when I got a call from my agent asking if I was interested in ghost-writing Willie's book. I had met him only once, fifteen years earlier, when his career ended ingloriously with the New York Mets. But this was to be an unusual writing arrangement, for Willie already had a ghost writer. The writer and Mays were longtime friends and the two had agreed to do the book. But the publisher, Simon and Schuster, wanted a writer with whom they were more familiar. Would I be willing to write the book from Willie's friend's manuscript—but not be listed as an author?

"Deep Ghost," I thought. Sounded intriguing. While I would have liked to see my name attached to Willie Mays's, the money was significant enough to stroke my ego.

Early on as a sportswriter, I learned to differentiate the playing-field persona from the public persona of athletes. There is also another persona that people who are on the "outside" do not see—the locker-room one. This is the relationship with sportswriters, even teammates. Some of the players like us. Some of them hate us, some distrust us, some are media hogs. And the truth is—we, the writers, quote the ones who love us. Often, we go for the easy interview. Hence, you may be reading your paper about your favorite team and wondering why a marginal player is quoted so often. The answer, usually, is that he or she is there, and available, and doesn't start off a conversation with, "What the heck do you want?"

Willie Mays had one of the best fan-friendly images in sports history. Repeatedly, he ranked near the top of TV-viewer credibility when advertisers took polls to find a spokesperson for their product. With good reason, I might add. He played with a joyous exuberance. He had a winning smile. As a rookie with the Giants, he got the nickname "Say Hey" because he couldn't remember people's names, so he shouted out "Say Hey" when he wanted someone's attention. It was part of his charm.

I dived into the writing project, hopeful of producing a big book, an important book. Certainly, there was enough meat—his career had begun in the Negro Leagues. At his retirement he and Hank Aaron were the last remaining players from those leagues. Mays had hit more home runs than any player before him, except for Babe Ruth. He had made legendary catches, throws, runs.

The first pages of the manuscript came to me with solid background information, but not much glitter or opinion. I forget how much money

Willie was getting for the book—I know it was in the six figures. I asked his collaborator to get me Willie's voice on many aspects of his life.

"I've only been able to see him twice," was the reply. "He's hard to get to."

Luckily, I know where to go for information. Beyond the record books, beyond the articles, there is a great historical source available to reporters virtually anywhere: a great library with extensive microfilm of old newspapers. So I went back to the 1950s to see stories in the seven newspapers that blanketed the city. The New York City Public Library on 42nd Street also has microfilm of many of America's other great papers—such as the *Chicago Tribune,* the *Washington Post,* the *St. Louis Post-Dispatch.*

For another perspective, I had come up with an interesting idea to gather facts and sidelights for previous biographies I had done. Rather than travel to every city where that person had made an impact, I called the sports editor of the major newspaper there, asked for the name of one of the clever interns or copy persons, and hired that person to go through that paper's clippings. So I was able to find out information about Mays's early years in Birmingham, Alabama, and his minor-league stint in St. Paul, Minnesota.

I finished Willie Mays's autobiography, about seventy thousand words, without ever speaking to Willie.

After mailing the final chapter to his agent, I left for San Diego and the Super Bowl. There, I got a call at my hotel. It was Willie's agent. "Willie likes the book very much," the agent told me. It was the first time I had heard Willie's opinion of the manuscript. "But he thinks he'd like the last chapter to show how he's grown as a person, how he's learned to accept a different kind of responsibility now that he's no longer an athlete."

That sounded like a fine idea. For the first time, I was given Willie's phone number so that we could make arrangements to get together. The week after the Super Bowl, he was playing in the Bing Crosby Pro-Am golf tournament up the coast in Pebble Beach. It was an easy hop from San Diego. I called Willie, and he was enthusiastic about talking about his post-baseball career, and how difficult it had been. He told me how he had to learn to keep appointments, how he no longer could rely on the club to give him a wake-up call to get somewhere, or to make travel arrangements for him. We agreed that he'd pick me up around noon at Tuesday at the airport near Carmel, California.

I arrived at the tiny airport ready to meet the new, responsible, Willie. Ten, fifteen, twenty minutes after landing I looked around. No Willie. Half an hour later, I called him.

"Willie?" I said.

"Who's this?" he replied.

"Jerry—Jerry Eskenazi," I said.

"Who?"

I explained I was the guy who was writing his book, and where was he? He got a bit agitated. He complained he had just gotten up, he had things to do, he had this and he had that. I told him there were no cabs around. I didn't even know where he was staying. He agreed to pick me up.

When celebrities play at these pro-am events, they are well cared for. Willie was given a house owned by a Pebble Beach member that over-looked the crashing waves below. Mays was given the family's Lincoln to use. Willie picked me up in the big car and we headed to his guest house. He had gotten over his annoyance at having to drive me and we had a good conversation. I took notes about how important he felt it was that athletes should learn responsibility.

As we snaked around the spectacular ocean drive, we suddenly came to a toll gate. A guard wearing a Smokey the Bear outfit told Mays there was a toll.

"I'm Willie Mays," said Willie. "Yeah, but you still have to pay," said the guard. "But I'm Willie Mays." This went back and forth—finally, exasper-ated, the Smokey told Willie to go through without paying the toll.

Finally settled down in the mansion—we were the only people in there—Willie actually was affable and interesting. We agreed that this last chapter would detail his road to becoming a person of substance. He told me how he had gotten a job as an official greeter for one hun-dred thousand dollars a year at Bally's in Atlantic City. His job was to play golf with the high rollers. Except that he was always late. Manage-ment called him on the carpet and he learned how to be on time.

He had other issues. In his last year with the Mets he was supposed to be a coach, but sometimes he left before the game had ended. The Mets were so annoyed at his slovenly work habits that someone actually kept a diary of Willie's comings and goings so that the club could get out of the contract. This had bothered Willie, who claimed the Mets were spying on him. But he learned from it, he said.

He detailed all this for me, and I was satisfied that we had finished the book on a note that was honest, and perhaps could serve as a cautionary tale for other athletes. It was dark outside by the time we finished, about seven o'clock. I asked him where in this five-bedroom sprawling mansion I could stay.

"Oh, you can't stay here," he said. "My wife's coming." Hmm.

I found the name of a nearby hotel, called for a cab, went back to New York the next day, and wrote the book. I never spoke to Willie again, although I heard he liked the last chapter.

Yastrzemski, on the other hand, was eager to talk. He even called me after our conversations and would remark, "Say, I thought of something interesting we should include." He took me out to Fenway Park one magical day to describe The Wall, the fabled Green Monster, and its peculiarities. This was all golden stuff, and fit in nicely with a theme he wanted me to play—how his career had been marked by hard work, how he had overcome his unimposing stature to become the only player in the history of the American League to amass three thousand hits and four hundred home runs with the same team.

His contract also called for him to do six appearances to promote the book. He did four in one day in New York City—and then it was sayonara. At the book signing at Barnes and Noble on Fifth Avenue in Rockefeller Center, he sold more books there than any author had previously. But after our whirlwind tour, I drove him to the LaGuardia shuttle to catch a flight to do Larry King's show in Washington. Next, I hoped, would be even more of Yaz's lucrative book signings and appearances in Boston. After all, that was where he had starred for more than twenty years with the Red Sox.

"Tell me, Jerry," said Yaz, who was pocketing $185,000 as an up-front advance. "How many books do we have to sell to start getting royalties?"

I told him—about forty thousand.

"Fuck it," was his literary reply. "We'll never sell that many. I don't think I'll do any more appearances."

* * *

Then there was Derek Sanderson. One night at the Playboy Club as we discussed what parts of the book we would delve into the next day, he put moves on our waitress, a Bunny. So much for our morning meeting.

Whenever I'd call him, be it noon, 10 A.M., early evening, I'd hear "Hello," in a voice that indicated he'd been sleeping just moments before. Once I went up to Boston, and was so annoyed he couldn't roll out of bed to start the interview that I walked out. His agent, Bob Woolf, called me and convinced me to finish.

Phil Esposito, on the other hand, was a pleasant small-town galoot. I wanted the first sentence of the book to read, "I'm a high school dropout," which to me was significant, because he had become the National Hockey League's leading scorer and a businessman in his own right. His agent took exception, thinking that a toothless hockey player's image would be hurt with that lead. I prevailed.

The Durocher and Veeck books actually were more interesting because these involved reconstructing lives of people I had never met, being written after their deaths, and called for real journalism and a dash of literary skill. Also diplomacy, since the widow Veeck had instructed everyone she knew not to talk to me because she was saving his life story to tell herself. For which I can't blame her, come to think of it.

Is there a bigger issue here? Perhaps it's that the living and the dead care about their images. Yaz was obsessed with keeping out of the book any suggestion his monster stage father was anything but a good ol' boy; Derek, the playboy hockey player, wanted everyone to know how clever he was; Phil Esposito was proud of his business acumen; Willie thought he had become a mensch.

As I contemplate all those bylines—besides the *Times,* they have appeared in publications ranging from *Cigar Aficionado,* to *Reader's Digest,* to the *Los Angeles Times,* and points in between, over more than four decades—I realize I have covered just about every assignment and worked under all conditions. The one exception has been Yom Kippur, the highest of the Jewish holidays.

But once, I almost did. And as the High Holy Days approach each year, I remind myself about keeping that day sacred—even from baseball, our National Pastime.

I was saved by Ron Blomberg. But I am getting ahead of my story.

Of course, Sandy Koufax is almost as famous in the Jewish community for eschewing to pitch on Yom Kippur as for the golden days on which he did pitch. A player who followed him many years later on the Dodgers, Shawn Green, also worked his way into Jewish hearts by making the same decision. The fact he also hit four home runs in a game didn't hurt his credibility, either.

For me, though, Blomberg is the Jewish ballplayer who always will matter most.

Back in 1971, when baseball games were played in little more than two hours, I foolishly told the *Times* I could work, even though Kol Nidre, heralding the start of Yom Kippur, was to be sung at 6 P.M. My office was stuck because of another reporter's illness. Well, I figured, the game gets under way at 1 P.M., over by 3:15, finish writing by 4:30, back on Long Island by 6—making Kol Nidre with a few minutes to spare.

Oy.

The Yankees were playing the Cleveland Indians that September day. Since we are taught as good little newspapermen that we are to be neutral, I didn't care who won—as long as I got out in time.

The Indians drew first blood, so to speak, with a run in the first inning. Good. Let someone score and let them win. I was a nonrooting observer. It didn't matter to me. But I got a pang when the Yankees tied the game in the third.

Then the Indians went ahead in the sixth. Great, I thought. But the unthinkable happened. The Yankees tied the game in the seventh. Well, still time enough before extra innings, I figured (rather, hoped), for someone to score a run and send me home. But no. No scoring in the eighth. No scoring the top of the ninth, and now we were in the bottom of the ninth. Yankees up. I was facing extra innings—and the shame of missing the most important night of the Jewish year.

I called home from the press box, repeatedly. I kept a running play-by-play with my wife, while she was getting dressed, while she was alternately giggling and sighing. I had most of my story written already—except for the "lead" and quotes about the winning play. Now, I prayed for a miracle to get me to the *shul* on time.

The Yankees had accumulated only two hits going into the ninth. They hadn't gotten one since the third inning. Extra innings seemed a certainty.

But as I look at the clipping now, it comes back to me: the Yankees got runners on first and third, one out, and Blomberg was coming to bat. Ron Blomberg. I always thought of him as more Georgian than Jewish. He had a country boy's way, a soft accent, a ready smile. Blomberg had been hitless in his three previous at-bats. Now, as he stepped to the plate, the sun (which was slowly sinking and making my angst even greater) was hidden behind an overcast sky. The Indians' manager told the outfield to play in because if Blomberg hit a deep fly, the runner at third would score anyway.

The moment was almost too much for me. I felt my worlds colliding. Here I was in the setting I had wanted since I was a child. But something even greater, almost a childhood fear that I would miss an important moment with my family, also gnawed.

Thank you, Ron Blomberg. He swung, and connected. The ball sailed into center field. I remember Vada Pinson looking at it soar over his head. Pinson slowly walked toward the Cleveland dugout, knowing the game had ended. The ball fell untouched. The winning run scored. Game over. Eskenazi was going to be home on time.

First, though, I had to get to the locker room to talk to Blomberg. Remember, this was late in the year, and the Yankees were going nowhere. Their revival as baseball's great franchise still was some years away.

Blomberg, though, was ecstatic.

"It's my day!" he shouted, noting it was the start of Yom Kippur. "Why do you think I did it? I knew sundown was coming. I could only stay another hour." In other words, he was going to go home before sundown? Yes, he said. His teammates were only vaguely aware of what he was talking about. He had never made any announcement about not playing on Yom Kippur. And anyway, he was no Koufax. But he was, after all, Jewish.

"I knew I was going to hit the ball, no matter what the pitcher threw," he contended. He had planned to leave, no matter what the situation was. "If the count had been 3-2, and the sun went down, I would have left," said Blomberg.

I threw in the quotes, polished off the story on my Olivetti portable, gave it to the Western Union guy who transcribed my story to the newspaper, and was off. I barreled down the Major Deegan Expressway, sped across the Long Island Expressway, got home about 5:40, sat down at the table where Roz and the kids were waiting. I made my prayer over bread and wine, the *bruchas,* wolfed down supper, changed my tie, and, smiling all the way, strolled over to the Shelter Rock Jewish Center in Roslyn, Long Island, with my family. A minute later, I heard Kol Nidre.

The next day's headline in the *Times* read, "Sundown Kid Hits Deadline Single."

Rabbi Myron Fenster, the powerful voice of our Temple, as well as a great sports fan, saw that headline as he read the paper before starting out for the synagogue. He decided to change his sermon. And he spoke to us about Blomberg's actions being a metaphor for Jewry, how all of us, when it comes down to us, think of our Jewishness.

I sat there listening, as proud of that story as any I have ever written. This was a convergence of my professional and private life. For the story I wrote was more than about sports. It was about a person's core. It was about Blomberg, but it also was about me. Indeed, Rabbi Fenster said it was about all of us.

The next time I saw Blomberg, a few weeks later, he was eating a ham sandwich.

But that's OK. It was a seminal moment for both of us. He was the Sundown Kid, and I learned that while you never can make a prediction in sports, you always know when Kol Nidre is and it's time to go home.

Other Books by Gerald Eskenazi

Gang Green: An Irreverent Look Behind the Scenes at Thirty-Eight (Well, Thirty-Seven) Seasons of New York Jets Football Futility

Bill Veeck: A Baseball Legend

The Lip: A Biography of Leo Durocher

Yaz (with Carl Yastrzemski)

A Year on Ice

Hockey

The Fastest Sport

There Were Giants in Those Days

A Thinking Man's Guide to Pro Soccer

Hockey Is My Life (with Phil Esposito)

The Derek Sanderson Nobody Knows

A Thinking Man's Guide to Pro Hockey

Hockey for Children

Miracle on Ice (with others)

The Way It Was (with others)